THE EARLIEST LIVES OF JESUS

THE EARLIEST
LIVES OF JESUS

R. M. Grant

LONDON

S·P·C·K

1961

First published in 1961
by S.P.C.K.
Holy Trinity Church
Marylebone Road
London N.W.1

Made and printed in Great Britain by
William Clowes and Sons, Limited, London and Beccles

CONTENTS

Page

1. THE GOSPELS IN THE FIRST TWO CENTURIES   1
   The Four Gospels   3
   Docetic-Gnostic Ideas   9
   Literary and Historical Criticism   14
   The Unity of the Gospels   30
   Clement of Alexandria   35

2. GREEK LITERARY AND HISTORICAL CRITICISM   38
   Literary and Historical Criticism: Theon   39
   Dio and Others   44
   Possible Alternatives   47

3. ORIGEN AND THE GOSPELS   50
   The Four Evangelists   52
   Inspiration and Contradiction   59
   The Johannine-Synoptic Contradictions   62
   A Different Approach—*Contra Celsum*   70

4. ORIGEN AND THE LIFE OF JESUS   80
   The Ministry and Person of Jesus   80
   Peter and his Confession   90
   From Galilee to Jerusalem   92
   The Passion Narrative   93
   The Crucifixion   95
   The Teaching of Jesus   98
   Eschatological Elements   107

Page

5. THE ENIGMA OF JESUS   III

    GLOSSARY   119

    1. ᾿Απομνημόνευμα, ἀπομνημονεύειν   119

    2. Ἱστορία   120

    3. Μῦθος   121

    4. Πλάσμα   123

APPENDIX: ORIGEN'S EXEGETICAL WRITINGS
    ON THE GOSPELS   124

BIBLIOGRAPHY   127

INDEXES:

Exegetical Terms   129

Biblical Passages Interpreted by Ancient Authors
    before Origen   130

Biblical Passages Interpreted by Origen   131

Ancient Authors or Literature   133

Modern Scholars   134

ABBREVIATIONS

ATR   *Anglican Theological Review*
HTR   *Harvard Theological Review*
JBL   *Journal of Biblical Literature*
JTS   *Journal of Theological Studies*
PG   *Patrologia graeca*
RE   *Real-Encyclopädie der classischen Altertumswissenschaft*
TU   *Texte und Untersuchungen*
ZNW   *Zeitschrift für die neutestamentliche Wissenschaft*

WORKS OF ORIGEN

C   *Contra Celsum*
E   *Exhortatio ad martyrium*
J   *Commentary on John*
L   *Homilies on Luke*
M   *Commentary on Matthew*
O   *De oratione*
P   *De principiis*
R   *Commentary on Romans*

METHOD OF CITATION

Greek rhetoricians are cited by volume, page, and line of the edition by L. Spengel, *Rhetores Graeci*, I–III (Leipzig, 1853–6); where no volume number is given, as often in the case of Theon, the reference is to volume II.

The works of Origen are cited as abbreviated above, with book, chapter, and section references as necessary (Greek Matthew with book and chapter, Latin Matthew with section), and the page number, in the Berlin edition when available, but otherwise in the edition of Lommatzsch or Migne.

PREFACE

THE PROBLEM of the way in which patristic exegetes viewed the New Testament, and indeed the whole Bible, has concerned scholars a good deal in recent years, especially since it has been discovered that many of the Fathers' methods were analogous to our own. The problem of historical criticism, however, does not seem to have occupied so much attention, though I should not fail to mention the work of Laeuchli, Daniélou, and the recent *Allegory and Event* by Hanson, which I have used in revising my own manuscript.

By concentrating on one problem, that of the life of Jesus, I have sought to see how early Christians up to and including Origen faced it, and what there is in their work which deserves retention or rejection.

The first chapter of this book was delivered in substance as a lecture in the autumn of 1957 at Union Theological Seminary, Brown University, the Philadelphia Divinity School, and the University of Chicago; it has been considerably revised since then. The whole book owes a good deal to the assistance given me by Professor Henry Chadwick and by my former student Professor W. R. Schoedel.

R. M. G.

The Divinity School,
University of Chicago

1

THE GOSPELS IN THE FIRST TWO CENTURIES

CONTEMPORARY New Testament critics are often rather proud of the degree to which they have been able to transcend the limitations of their predecessors, who lost themselves in minute details of textual, literary, and historical criticism and tried to find out something about the life of Jesus. Though there is considerable evidence that what has been contemporary is so no longer, the "contemporary" or almost contemporary attitude is so widespread that it deserves a little criticism.

The attitude seems to be based on two presuppositions. First, the "faith" or the proclamation of the "kerygma" was not really related to historical evidence. This presupposition can be supported to some extent by isolated verses from the Pauline epistles in which Paul is exaggerating the extent of his independence from the Church of Jerusalem. It can hardly be justified by the synoptic gospels or, for that matter, by John 20.30–1.

> Now Jesus did many other signs in the presence of his disciples, which are not written in this book; but these are written so that you may believe that Jesus is the Christ, the Son of God, and that by believing you may have life in his name.

Faith is not based on faith, or simply on events as events, but on the historical record of events, as in Paul's list of resurrection appearances and witnesses in 1 Cor. 15.

Second, literary and historical criticism are the creations of modern "rationalism". In the golden age of primitive faith, no one paid any attention to the literary and historical problems which the true believer ignored; only with the infiltration of Greek or Graeco-Roman conceptions into the pure stream of Hebrew-Christian revelation did such problems arise. Such a presupposition is based on the severance of the primitive Church from what succeeded it, on the sharp differentiation of "Hebrew" from "Greek" ideas, and upon all the host of related notions invented in order to create the notion that early Church history is nothing but a story of decline and fall.

In my opinion, both presuppositions are false, and it is the purpose of this book to show how the problems, historical in nature, which arise out of the canonical gospels whenever they are thoughtfully considered were faced by Christian writers in the first two or three centuries. I should not claim perfection for the methods, often borrowed from the Greek schools, which they followed, or for the results they achieved by using them. All I intend to do is to look carefully and critically at the procedures and achievements of the early Church Fathers, in the belief that we can learn something from them in regard not only to questions they themselves emphasized but also to questions, like that of writing the life of Jesus, which they did not emphasize. In other words, I am going to ask them a modern question, in the hope that the materials they provide will supply something of an answer to it. There is no reason to suppose that in historical matters their minds worked entirely differently from our own.

It must be admitted, however, that by asking a modern question we are likely to get a modernized answer. Ancient Christians had in mind a picture of a person with a "historical" life, but they were not primarily interested in dealing with that life either by using any psychological techniques or by employing historical tools to analyse the setting in time and place. They did not ask themselves, as we might ask ourselves of any historical character, what it was his nature to be and to do. They did not try to make Jesus comprehensible against his environment in the manner of a modern biographer. And once they had decided not only that Jesus himself was the divine logos but also that the sources for his life were written under divine inspiration, all the presuppositions which might make a "biographical" interest possible had disappeared.[1]

In spite of these difficulties we shall try to move back and forth

[1] For this paragraph I am indebted to Professor Henry Chadwick.

from ancient to modern times in the hope that some of the results will perhaps illuminate ideas held in both periods.

THE FOUR GOSPELS

Any attempt to recover the historical life of Jesus depends upon an analysis of the four gospels, of their interrelations, and of their sources. Analysis of the gospels themselves as literary documents means that we endeavour to observe and to understand what the individual evangelists say and how they say it; if possible, we may even be able to discover why they say what they say. Study of their interrelations means that we examine the extent to which Matthew, Mark, and Luke agree and the extent to which they disagree, in relation to matters of arrangement, of style, and of vocabulary, and try to explain both agreements and disagreements. Turning from these three gospels, called "synoptic" because to such a considerable extent they can be viewed together, we pass to the fourth gospel, which because of its unique arrangement and viewpoint, not to mention its content as a whole, has to be treated separately. When we consider the sources of the gospels we try to determine the extent to which any one of the evangelists may have made use of earlier documents (possibly including others of the gospels which we possess) and, behind such documents, various oral traditions or cycles of tradition which were in existence long before he wrote.

Like most of the early Fathers, we do not consider apocryphal gospels (those not preserved in the canon of the New Testament) or "unwritten sayings" as reliable sources for information about the life of Jesus. Too little control was exercised over the composition or transmission of these materials for us to be able to use them with any degree of confidence.

It is obvious that modern historical analysis of the gospels is somewhat different from the analysis provided in the early Church. The difference is due to several factors of varying importance. In the first place, the questions about authorship which have been raised, chiefly in modern times, mean that many of the questions we ask rarely entered the minds of the Fathers. In the patristic view, two of our gospels were written by apostles; the

3

other two were written by disciples of the apostles. Matthew and John were thus eyewitnesses to the events they described, while Mark derived his information from Peter, Luke from Paul. This traditional hypothesis meant that no questions could be asked about the sources, or possible sources, employed by either Matthew or John. The differences between these two gospels had to be explained exclusively by attempts to interpret the purposes which their authors had in view. In the second place, at least at Alexandria great emphasis was laid on the mantic inspiration of the evangelists, who by creating disagreements among their gospels were trying to lead their readers toward allegorical exegesis. In origin this theory may well have been intended to explain why there were disagreements of various kinds; but it tended to drive exegetes not to explain disagreements but to explain them away. Finally, when the Fathers dealt with literary and historical problems in the gospels they employed the methods traditionally taught in Greek schools of rhetoric. These methods could satisfactorily lead to the classification of literary forms and even to the assessment of degrees of credibility. Their use, however, meant that literary interrelations and the employment of sources could not be adequately handled. What was lacking was genuine historical criticism.

We shall see that even in the work of Origen, greatest of the early Christian exegetes, there is a failure to come to grips with the historical problem of the life of Jesus. In part this failure is due to Origen's Christological doctrine, in which the Incarnation is verbally accepted but effectively neglected; in part it is due to the methods of rhetorical analysis which he used. The two complement each other.

Before coming to Origen, however, we must look at some of the problems present in the gospels and see how they were faced or ignored by Christian writers before his time; then we shall deal with his own work in relation to some of the more important questions involved in writing a life of Jesus.

All three synoptic gospels begin the story of Jesus' public ministry with accounts of the mission of John the Baptist, of Jesus' baptism by him and the descent of the Spirit and the words of a voice from heaven; then comes the account of the temptation in the wilderness, the arrest of John by Herod, preaching in Galilee, and the call of the first disciples. All three include the feeding of the five thousand, Peter's confession, Jesus' prediction of his own death, and his transfiguration. All three provide the story of the last journey to Jerusalem, the triumphal entry, the cleansing of the temple, teaching in and near Jerusalem (largely apocalyptic), the last supper, the Gethsemane scene, and the rest of the passion narrative. Their accounts of resurrection appearances are somewhat different. Matthew explicitly locates them in Galilee; Mark does so by implication; but Luke places them near Jerusalem.

Now when we turn from the synoptic gospels to John, we find a picture quite different in character. There is no infancy narrative; instead, John provides a theological prologue concerning the divine Logos. Next he tells of John the Baptist; he insists that he was not the Christ and does not mention Jesus' baptism by him; then he describes the call of the first disciples in Galilee. This event is followed by Jesus' changing water into wine at a wedding in Cana, a visit to Capernaum, and a journey to Jerusalem for the cleansing of the temple. John explicitly states (3.24) that the Baptist had not yet been imprisoned. Toward the middle of Jesus' ministry we find the feeding of the five thousand and something like Peter's confession, but there is no explicit prediction of Jesus' death, and no transfiguration. Jesus visits Jerusalem several times, not once as in the synoptics. The triumphal entry is not followed by the cleansing of the temple, an event which John has placed early in Jesus' ministry, and the words of institution are omitted, since John has paraphrased them in his account of the meaning of the feeding of the five thousand. The last supper, treated as a Passover meal by the synoptists, is not so regarded by John, who has Jesus crucified on the day of preparation for the Passover (18.28; 19.14). There is no Gethsemane scene. The synoptists have Simon of Cyrene carry Jesus' cross; according to John, Jesus himself carried it. The resurrection appearances take place in Jerusalem; only the appendix to John (21.1–23) describes an appearance in Galilee.

Apart from these differences related to events, there is also a difference between the teaching of Jesus as reported in the synoptics and the long Johannine discourses, which deal chiefly with the revelation of the Father through the Son. Only one such saying is preserved by the synoptic evangelists (Matt. 11.25–7; Luke 10.21–2). Without great exaggeration one can say that while the synoptists describe Jesus' proclamation of the imminent coming, or the inauguration, of the kingdom of God, John tells of the meaning of the revelation of the Son of God. It is hard to believe that, historically considered, both accounts of Jesus can be correct. And if the early Christian tradition that John wrote last is reliable, his gospel contains a theological meditation on the meaning of the Jesus described, and perhaps misunderstood, in the earlier gospels.

It is at this point that the problem of whether John knew the synoptic gospels or not becomes important. In recent years there have been several advocates of the hypothesis that he did not know them but drew on traditions partly like those they used, partly unlike them.[1] On the other hand, Windisch presented strong arguments on behalf of the theory that he wrote in order to supplant the synoptic gospels, which he knew.[2] And Bultmann has argued that most of the passages which have synoptic parallels are the work of an ecclesiastical redactor, determined to make the gospel acceptable in churches which used the synoptic gospels.[3] One may also mention the claim that affinities between John and the Dead Sea Scrolls prove that his gospel was written early;[4] it is hard to see what validity such a claim can have, for we know that Dead Sea documents were employed by Christians writing no earlier than the second century.[5]

The most likely solution of the problem seems to be that John's gospel is actually independent of the synoptics; he did

---

[1] P. Gardner-Smith, *St John and the Synoptic Gospels* (Cambridge, 1938); E. R. Goodenough in *JBL* 64 (1945), pp. 145–82; cf. also pp. 535–44 (R. P. Casey and Goodenough).

[2] H. Windisch, *Johannes und die Synoptiker* (Leipzig, 1926).

[3] R. Bultmann, *Das Evangelium des Johannes* (Göttingen, 1941).

[4] R. E. Brown in K. Stendahl, *The Scrolls and the New Testament* (New York, 1957), p. 206; F. M. Cross, Jr, *The Ancient Library of Qumran* (New York, 1958), pp. 161–2.

[5] Cf. M. de Jonge, *The Testaments of the Twelve Patriarchs* (Assen, 1953).

not use them among his sources. To date his gospel, however, is practically impossible. It probably comes from a time considerably before the end of the first century.

John's independence does not, however, mean that his record of events is more reliable than that of the other evangelists. The fact that his theology, like that of Paul, influenced the later Church more strongly than that of the synoptists is no guarantee of his work as an historian. And the anonymous statement at the end of his gospel, "This is the disciple who bears witness of these things, and wrote these things; and we know that his witness is true" (21.24), provides us with little information, since we do not know that by "true" is meant "historically accurate" (contrast Luke 1.3–4).

How do the evangelists actually know the words and deeds they report? Here it is significant that Mark represents the disciples as failing to comprehend some of the essential points of Jesus' teaching. They do not understand the inner meaning of parables and have to have them explained privately (4.13,34). They do not understand the meaning of the miraculous feedings of the five and four thousand (6.52; 8.16–21). And they cannot understand what Jesus means by foretelling resurrection after suffering (8.32–3; 9.32; 10.32–45). Both Luke and Matthew modify the disciples' understanding of parables; Luke omits most of the relevant materials, while Matthew adds (13.51) a significant bit of dialogue. "Have you understood all these things? They say to him, Yes." Luke omits all the material dealings with failure to understand the feeding, while Matthew, once more, alters it at some points (especially 14.33). As for the passion-predictions, Luke retains them, generally speaking, while Matthew omits, contradicts (17.23), or modifies them (20.20–8).

It is plain enough that the tendency after Mark is to soften the picture of the disciples' ignorance found in the earliest gospel. But it must be remembered that Mark himself is well aware of what the true teaching is—the true teaching on the grounds of which he can criticize the disciples' ignorance. And if he knows it, it must have become clear at some time after the earthly ministry of Jesus. It would be natural to assume that he knew the true

7

teaching because of the resurrection and the gift of the Spirit.

What is implicit in Mark and the other synoptics becomes explicit in the fourth gospel, where we find at two significant points that emphasis is laid on the disciples' remembering and interpreting earlier events. The first passage is that concerned with the cleansing of the temple. After the cleansing, "his disciples remembered that it was written, 'Zeal for thy house will consume me'" (John 2.17). After a discussion of Jesus' words after the cleansing, John goes on to say that, "When therefore he was raised from the dead, his disciples remembered that he had said this; and they believed the scripture and the word which Jesus had spoken" (2.22). A similar description of creative remembering is found in relation to the triumphal entry. Jesus enters on a colt and fulfils a prophecy in Zechariah: "his disciples did not understand this at first, but when Jesus was glorified, then they remembered that this had been written of him and had been done to him" (12.16). Since John, unlike the synoptic evangelists, has separated the triumphal entry from the cleansing of the temple,[1] he may be suggesting that his own chronology is right. Or he may be insisting on the importance of reflective meditation in the transmission of tradition. In any event, the "remembering" of the disciples is no merely human activity. John explicitly teaches that it is the Holy Spirit who, after the resurrection, teaches the disciples all things and brings to their remembrance all that Jesus taught them (14.26). This Spirit of Truth leads Christians into all the truth (15.13).

If John knew the synoptic gospels, then, he would have regarded them as inferior to his own work, for they reflect a standpoint earlier than the resurrection and therefore inadequate. To be sure, Luke tried to write history. He constantly refers to witnesses to the life, death, and resurrection of Jesus.[2] But his

---

[1] Luke apparently places them on the same day, while Mark and Matthew have a night intervene.

[2] Luke 1.2; 24.48; Acts 1.8,22; 2.32; 3.15; 4.33; 5.32; 10.36–43. Since the ordinary text of Luke 22.19–20 is close to 1 Cor. 11.23–5, ancient readers might assume that Luke's information came from Paul, Paul's (as he says) "from the Lord".

gospel is not a product of creative reminiscence as John's is. The fourth gospel is the only gospel explicitly based on post-resurrection reinterpretation.

It is also the only gospel which represents itself as the work of an eyewitness to the life of Jesus. Neither Mark nor Matthew has anything to say about authorship; it may be the mention of the name Matthew in Matthew 9.9 ("Levi" in the parallels, Mark 2.13 and Luke 5.27) which led ancient critics to ascribe the gospel to him. Luke explicitly claims to follow eyewitnesses, not to be an eyewitness himself (1.2–3). But of the Word of God the evangelist says that he "dwelt among us" and "we beheld his glory" (1.14), a glory manifested in the signs worked before the disciples (2.11). Who is the evangelist? In this gospel as not in the synoptics there is a mysterious "disciple whom Jesus loved" (13.23–5), who takes Mary to his own house (19.26–7) and first reaches the empty tomb (20.4). It is probably this disciple who "was known to the high priest" (18.15) and witnessed the coming of blood and water from Jesus' side (19.34–5). And at least according to the epilogue to the gospel, this disciple wrote the book (21.24). Who was he? Various answers have been given. "Tradition" suggests that he was John the son of Zebedee, but this conjecture has nothing to commend it. A more likely guess, based on the gospel itself, would be that the author was Nicodemus. Nicodemus had a private conversation with Jesus which is reported in the gospel (3.1–15 or 3.1–21); as a Pharisee, he was known to the high priest (7.50); and he was in Jerusalem at the time of the crucifixion (19.39–42). We may not be able to tell who the author actually was, but it is important to note that he seems to regard himself as an eyewitness. For this reason, as well as because of his concern for theology, early Christians valued his work highly.

Docetic-Gnostic Ideas

Historical analysis did not arise in the course of the earliest controversies. Instead, in the early second century we find theological exegetes of doubtful orthodoxy insisting that Jesus, or more properly the Christ, since he was a divine being, was not born, did not suffer, and did not die. When Ignatius, Bishop of Antioch, insisted, in opposition to such persons, that Jesus "truly" did various things he did not enter into the question of historical evidence, since they did not raise it. Genuine debate could take place only when specific pieces of evidence were brought into the dispute.

A relatively early example of such specific evidence is provided in Irenaeus' account of the teaching of the gnostic Basilides.[1] According to this account, Basilides held that Jesus was not actually crucified because Simon of Cyrene took his place. Such an opinion seems ridiculous at first glance. But if we look at the gospel of Mark we see that while the author clearly intended to describe the crucifixion of Jesus, his words can be understood as referring to the crucifixion of Simon (Mark 15.21–5). And it appears that the later evangelists found Mark's account inadequate. According to Mark, the title on the cross read "King of the Jews" (15.26); Matthew changes it to "This is Jesus, king of the Jews" (27.37). Luke adds that Simon carried the cross behind Jesus (23.26), and John does not mention Simon but says that Jesus carried his own cross (19.17). This gnostic interpretation shows how severely literal gnostic exegesis could be, and how embarrassing it became to its opponents. On the other hand, alterations made in order to avoid one kind of difficulty could produce further difficulties, once the original occasion of the alterations was forgotten; for the stories of the crucifixion are now different in the various gospels.

A real exegetical crisis was produced in the Roman Church about the year 137, when a certain Marcion came from Pontus by the Black Sea and proceeded to argue not only that the authentic gospel contradicted the Old Testament (such a view was familiar from the teaching of earlier gnostics) but also that there was only one authentic gospel, at first transmitted orally, then put into writing and severely interpolated by enthusiasts for Judaism. Upon examination, this gospel proves to have been that traditionally ascribed to Luke; but Marcion presented it in a form

[1] *Adv. haer.* I, 24, 4, p. 200, Harvey.

considerably reduced by the removal of what he regarded as interpolations.

We need not pay too much attention to the many minor changes which Marcion made in the gospel of Luke, for the major ones clearly indicate the purpose he had in mind.[1] His gospel began with the words, "In the fifteenth year of Tiberius [Luke 3.1a] the saving Spirit Jesus came down to Capernaum [Luke 4.31]."[2] Thus he omitted the stories of Jesus' conception, birth, infancy, baptism, genealogy, temptation, preaching, and rejection at Nazareth. His gospel was therefore more like John than like Matthew and Mark, since among these items John records only the baptism, and he severely modifies the story. Such deletions would be appropriate in telling the story of a "saving spirit" or divine being, as Origen later suggests in regard to the fourth gospel. The other extensive omission is that of Luke 19.29–46: preparation for the entry into Jerusalem, the triumphal entry itself, Jesus' lament over Jerusalem, and the cleansing of the temple. Because of his hostility toward Judaism, Marcion did not like the notion that Jesus entered Jerusalem as its king and cleansed the temple there. But he may also have been aware that in John the cleansing is placed early rather than late in Jesus' ministry. He may have been given theological assistance by this chronological difficulty. In other words, at least at these two key points Marcion's gospel was synoptic in content but Johannine in framework.[3]

In Marcion's opinion Jesus had proclaimed a completely novel (in other words, non-Jewish) gospel which was corrupted by his Jewish disciples because they were slaves of tradition. This gospel was given again by revelation to Paul, whose letters were once more corrupted and interpolated. When properly corrected, however, they could serve as the key to the recovery of the true gospel. Marcion knew from his reading of the Pauline epistles that there had been a conflict between Paul and the more

---

[1] For his theological presuppositions cf. *The Letter and the Spirit*, pp. 115–19.

[2] He retained other verses from Luke 4 but rearranged them; cf. A. v. Harnack, *Marcion: das Evangelium vom fremden Gott* (2nd ed., Leipzig, 1924), pp. 183*–7*.

[3] For an attempt to solve the difficulty cf. O. Cullmann, *The Early Church* (Philadelphia, 1956), pp. 59–75.

Judaistic apostles of Jerusalem, especially James and Peter. And he knew that the apostle had received his gospel not from any man but by means of a revelation of Jesus Christ (Gal. 1.12). In 2 Cor. 12 he could read that Paul received a great many revelations, and from 1 Cor. 11.23 he could conclude that among them was the story of the last supper, since the only gospel was the authentic one which Paul had received. Yet Luke is not Pauline. It therefore had to be made Pauline, or semi-Pauline, by the removal of Judaizing interpolations. The basic ground of Marcion's work, then, was the Pauline doctrine, or part of the Pauline doctrine, which he found in parts of the major Pauline epistles. Either he did not know Acts and the pastoral epistles or else he rejected them. We have already suggested that he may have known something like the gospel of John and was able to use it for the framework of the life of Jesus.

The method Marcion employed is found among Graeco-Roman grammarians who believed that they were able to separate mythological additions from ancient theological texts. These additions had been made by poets in order to charm their readers or by priests in the interest of their own superstitions.[1] Marcion's theory is similar to that of the grammarians. In his view, Jewish apostles and others made additions in order to Judaize the gospel. We do not know whether he offered any proof for this theory or not. But since no evidence against it was available, his "heresy" created a sensation in the Roman Church and elsewhere. He was expelled from the Roman community.

Marcion had regarded Church history as the story of interpolation, or in other words the story of decline and fall. At Rome about the same time, the Valentinians interpreted it in the light of the ultimate gospel, their own Gospel of Truth; and they proceeded to interpret the other gospels allegorically so that the same doctrine could be found in all. In the school of Valentinus we find an attempt to classify the words and deeds of Jesus, ostensibly in relation to their form but really in relation to their content. The Valentinian Theodotus tells us that Jesus taught his disciples "at first, typically and mystically; later, parabolically

[1] *The Letter and the Spirit*, pp. 19–25.

12

and enigmatically; and thirdly, clearly and plainly, in private".[1] This scheme is presumably based on the gospels. There we read that Jesus' first sign involved the transformation of water from Jewish water-pots into wine (John 2.1–11). Later he taught his disciples in dark sayings (John 16.25) or in parables (Mark 4.33–4). Finally he spoke openly to them, when they were alone (John 16.25,29; cf. Mark 4.34).

The difference between public and private teaching was further emphasized by another Valentinian teacher. He held that Jesus secretly taught only those disciples who were able to understand "arguments, enigmas, and parables". In this way he taught them about the true Father, but elsewhere he used the term "God" to refer to the Demiurge or God of the Old Testament.[2] This point too is based on the gospels, where the term "Father" is used by Jesus only when he is alone with his disciples.

The Valentinian conception, then, involves a contrast between public teaching not literally true and private teaching which is genuinely theological. It also involves belief in the disciples' progressive understanding of the meaning of Jesus' ministry, an understanding presumably culminating in the theology of Valentinus himself.

With this exegetical key, the Valentinians proved to be remarkably subtle exegetes of Jesus' teaching, especially of his parables, which had already been treated as allegories by the synoptic evangelists. Ptolemaeus was able to read the doctrine of the heavenly aeons into the prologue of the fourth gospel, and Heracleon provided exegetical notes on at least the first eight chapters of the gospel. Heracleon was well aware of some of the stylistic difficulties in John. For example, he argues that while John 1.15–17 was quoted from John the Baptist, the following verse ("No one has ever seen God . . .") is a comment by the evangelist. Origen disagreed with him sharply, ascribing the whole section to the Baptist.[3] Actually, both commentators were wrong, since the evangelist's statements begin with John 1.16. But the fact that Heracleon was able to see a difficulty shows that he possessed the critical eye indispensable for the allegorist.

[1] Clement, *Exc. ex Theod.* 66.   [2] Irenaeus, *Adv. haer.* 2, 27, 3, p. 348.   [3] *J* 6, 2, p. 109.

Both Marcionites and Valentinians presented grave difficulties to the majority of early Christians, unaccustomed to read the gospels with such subtle criticisms in view. Both philology and historical criticism were practically unknown in Christianity before the rise of gnostic teachers. But as a result of this gnostic exegesis, it became necessary for Christians to present some literary and historical defence of the gospels. Examples of this new way of looking at things are to be found in the writings of Papias and Justin.

LITERARY AND HISTORICAL CRITICISM

Marcionites and Valentinians made trouble for their fellow-Christians by insisting that they possessed the true text of the gospel or the true exegesis of the gospel, or both. When Christians who were less heterodox tried to refute such claims, they were inevitably driven to make use of the critical methods taught in the grammatical and rhetorical schools of their time. Their use of these methods is not surprising, since those Christians who wrote books had almost certainly been educated in the schools. Jesus may (or may not) have been self-taught, but it is certain that the New Testament writers had learned how to write in schools, and that at least Paul, Luke, and the authors of 1–2 Peter, Hebrews, and James were acquainted with Greek rhetoric. Furthermore, the preface to Luke-Acts shows that its author stood, and intended to stand, in the tradition of Greek historical writing.[1] He tells us that he has had "many" predecessors, that he himself had followed everything carefully (ἀκριβῶς) for some time past, and that he is writing an orderly (καθεξῆς) account by means of which certainty may be attained (Luke 1.1–4). Marcion omitted this statement from his version of Luke, presumably because no emphasis on divine inspiration is to be found in it; besides, it refers to other gospel writings.

The first task which had to be undertaken by Christians who

---

[1] Theon tells us that the historian should mention his subject's ancestors and parents and note the Olympiads in which an Olympic victor won (83.29—84.1); Luke, unlike Mark, tells about the genealogy of Jesus (3.23–38), names his parents (1.27), and dates the mission of John the Baptist (3.1–2).

wanted to discuss the gospels was that of classifying them and their materials. Naturally enough, they used the classifications already available in the manuals composed by Graeco-Roman rhetoricians. Here they could find, apart from forms likely to be found only in rhetorical addresses, about five classifications which could be used in connection with the gospels or what was in them. Theon, who wrote his *Progymnasmata* early in the second century of our era, gives definitions and descriptions of myth (a false account portraying truth), narrative (an account descriptive of events which took place or might have taken place), and χρεία (a brief declaration or action referred to some definite person or to something like a person). The χρεία, says Theon, resembles both a proverbial saying (γνώμη) and an ἀπομνημόνευμα, but in some respects it is different from both. It is different from a proverbial saying because (1) it always refers to a particular person; (2) it is not always general in nature; (3) it does not always give a moral lesson; and (4) it is not always simply a saying. It is different from an ἀπομνημόνευμα because (1) it is shorter and (2) it always refers to a particular person.[1] Theon provides an elaborate classification of χρεῖαι,[2] but other rhetoricians, such as Hermogenes, regarded it as unnecessarily complicated,[3] and we do not need to discuss it at this point.

A Christian scholar of the second century would inevitably deny that the gospels had anything to do with the category of myth. He might well suggest that they were historical narratives (διηγήσεις) which contained historical materials (διηγήματα).[4] But actually what our earliest witnesses had in mind was that the gospels were ἀπομνημονεύματα, materials worked up from χρεῖαι and γνῶμαι. In this way they were indirectly pointing toward the oral origin of the gospel traditions. Papias, Bishop of Hierapolis in Asia Minor early in the second century, himself relied on oral tradition and stated that it was preferable to written documents.[5] He described Mark's work with the verb ἀπομνημονεύειν;[6]

---

[1] Pp. 72.28; 78.15; 96.19—97.6.   [2] Pp. 97.11—101.2.   [3] P. 6.15 (7.10 Rabe).
[4] This distinction is drawn by Hermogenes, p. 4.21 (4.9 Rabe).
[5] Papias preferred the "living voice" of tradition; cf. Quintilian, *Inst.* 2, 2, 7.
[6] Eusebius, *H.E.* 3, 39, 15.

similarly Justin, who wrote at Rome about 150, classified the gospels as the ἀπομνημονεύματα of the apostles.[1]

Papias did not confine his historical studies to an analysis of literary forms. He tells us, in a passage preserved by Eusebius,[2] that he engaged in historical investigations which took him back to the first generation of Christian disciples.

> If someone happened to come along who had been a follower of the elders, I investigated his words—in regard to what Andrew or Peter or Philip or Thomas, or James or John or Matthew, or any other of the Lord's disciples, had said, or what Aristion and the elder John, the Lord's disciples, were saying.

Here we can probably differentiate two stages of tradition. The first group of seven disciples belongs to the earliest times of Christianity, to the apostolic generation itself. The next two names, those of Aristion and John, presumably are those of older contemporaries of Papias. The difficulty with Papias' words lies in the fact that he seems both to differentiate elders from disciples and at the same time to identify them. Since elsewhere, however, he calls his own informants "elders", it would appear that in general he recognized a difference between the two groups.

But who were the disciples of Jesus whose sayings were being reported? It is fairly obvious that Papias' list is based primarily upon the apostles or disciples named in the gospel of John. It is there, and only there that we meet, in the same order, Andrew (1.40), Peter (1.40–2), Philip (1.43), and Thomas (11.16). In the synoptic lists of apostles their names are never found in this order. We must therefore conclude that Papias knew either the gospel of John or its author, and perhaps both.

The fact that he knows John is confirmed by what he says about his own writing.[3]

> I did not take pleasure in those who say much, as the many do, but in those who teach the truth; nor did I record alien commandments but, instead, those given by the Lord to the faith and derived from the Truth itself.

Here he is criticizing the rise of false gospels in the light of his own tradition derived from the Jesus who was himself the Truth

---

[1] See p. 20 below.   [2] *H.E.* 3, 39, 4.   [3] Eusebius, *H.E.* 3, 39, 3.

(John 14.6). He may think that the apocryphal gospels are unduly lengthy. He may be emphasizing this point because he remembers that brevity is the soul of the χρεία-form which Jesus and his disciples used.[1]

His remarks about Matthew are not altogether unambiguous. He tells us that Matthew compiled either the oracles of Jesus or (less probably) the oracles about Jesus in a Hebrew dialect; afterwards, various translations were made into Greek. This statement presumably means that in Papias' time there were several Greek gospels which claimed the authority of Matthew. One of them was probably our gospel of Matthew; another may have been the gospel according to the Hebrews, which often resembles it. Papias was unwilling to choose between, or among, them. The fact that "each reader translated as he was able" suggests that the authority of the gospel had been considerably diminished by the diversity in the translations.

In discussing Mark, Papias does no more than to reproduce what "the elder John" had told him. Mark's gospel goes back in substance to the disciple Peter, whose translator Mark was.

> Mark, who was an interpreter of Peter, wrote down accurately whatever he recorded of what had been either said or done by the Lord, but ⟨his account was⟩ by no means in order. For he neither heard nor followed the Lord, but later, as I said, ⟨he heard and followed⟩ Peter.

The disorder of Mark's gospel is thus due to the circumstances under which Mark wrote—and also to the way in which Peter taught.[2]

> Peter gave his teachings in χρεία-form; he was not making a compilation (σύνταξις) of the dominical oracles.

In this way Peter differed from Matthew, who did make such a σύνταξις.

> Therefore Mark was not wrong when he wrote down single items in the form of ἀπομνημονεύματα ὡς ἀπομνηόνευσεν. For he had one purpose in mind; not to leave out anything he heard or to tell anything falsely among these items.

[1] Cf. Theon, p. 96.19; Hermogenes, p. 5.26 (6.5 Rabe).
[2] For this translation of χρεία cf. R. O. P. Taylor, *The Groundwork of the Gospels* (Oxford, 1946), pp. 75–90.

Obviously the elder is admitting the force of criticisms which have been made of Mark's gospel. At the same time he is trying to explain them away in relation to the circumstances under which Mark wrote and the purpose he had in view.

Mark's gospel is not a σύνταξις, a finished product of rhetorical art. It is an ἀπομνημόνευμα or a collection of ἀπομνημονεύματα based on the traditions which had already been shaped into χρεῖαι by Peter. Now according to the rules laid down by the rhetoricians, a χρεία can be criticized on the grounds (among others) that it leaves things out or that what it tells is false.[1] It cannot be criticized for its lack of order, because it has no special order. The fact that the elder and Papias clearly indicate that Mark's gospel has the virtues of truth and of relative completeness, while it does not have the order which was in any case unnecessary, shows that they were examining the gospel from the standpoint of Greek literary criticism.[2]

Now if we trace the process of composition and analysis from the beginning onwards, we see that there were originally memories and oral traditions about what Jesus had said and done. These were given shape in χρεία-form by the apostle Peter, and doubtless by others as well. The χρεῖαι which came from Peter were recorded by his disciple Mark, who intended to preserve all that Peter taught and to preserve it accurately. Whether he was successful or not, we do not know. He did not produce a finished composition, for his gospel lacks arrangement, whether chronological or literary or both. If the elder John was the author of the fourth gospel, he must have believed that his own book did possess a correct order. And to judge from Papias' relation to the gospel of John, he must have held the same view. But Papias must also have valued his own work highly. It was as close to the authentic oral tradition as the gospels of Mark and Luke; unlike Matthew, it was written in Greek. Unfortunately it was

---

[1] Theon, p. 104.15–18.

[2] According to Weinel (*RE* XIV, 1858) not more than the first sentence about Mark comes from the elder John; "as I said" shows that Papias is giving his own adaptation of the elder's remarks. F. C. Grant (*The Earliest Gospel*, New York, 1943, pp. 34–7) also ascribes much of the information to Papias' revision, but does not separate the two sources so sharply. Neither do I.

not preserved by many of the Christian churches and is now lost.

As a historian, Papias regarded the work of the evangelists as not unlike his own. He cannot have believed that they possessed some special gift of inspiration for their writing, since he describes Mark's efforts in purely historical terms. He may well have believed that John's gospel was more closely related to the Truth who was Jesus, but if this inference is correct he valued John's closeness to historical events more than any inspiration he may have been given as an evangelist.

Almost exactly the same kind of analysis of the gospels and their sources is to be found in the writings of the apologist Justin shortly after the middle of the second century. Critics have often regarded Justin as a rather inept philosophical theologian, and he himself describes some of the gaps in his philosophical education. But when he lists the subjects with which his acquaintance was slight, he does not include grammar and rhetoric among them.[1] From his writings we should assume that he had some training in a school of rhetoric. Such training seems to be reflected in what he says about the Christian books.

In Justin's opinion, the sayings of Jesus were "brief and concise" because he was not a sophist, a speaker devoted to words for their own sake.[2] What Justin has in mind is the form of the sayings in the sermon on the mount, from which he gives some quotations. In other words, for him the sayings are γνῶμαι, short sententious sayings characteristic of "gnomic" poets or philosophers. "A gnome", says Hermogenes, "is a summary statement given in a general declaration, discouraging or recommending something or explaining the nature of each kind of action."[3] Since it was gnomic, Jesus' teaching was more luminous than the sun,[4] even though on some occasions his words were "veiled"— as when he spoke about the "sign of Jonah" (Matt. 16.4).[5] Presumably Justin regarded the parables as "veiled" too; and he makes practically no allusions to them.[6]

[1] Dial. 2, 4; cf. JTS N.S. 7 (1956), pp. 246–8.   [2] Apol. 1, 14, 5; cf. Dial. 18, 1.
[3] II, 7, 12 Spengel (8, 16 Rabe).   [4] Dial. 121, 2.
[5] Dial. 107, 1; for similar speech in the Old Testament cf. Dial. 52, 1; 76, 2 and 6.
[6] A. Jülicher, Die Gleichnisreden Jesu I (2nd ed., Tübingen, 1910), pp. 210–11.

What of the accounts of Jesus' life? Outsiders might suppose that the stories about him are like myths composed by poets and are nothing but wonder stories (τερατολογία).[1] They would be wrong if they made such an analysis, first because the life of Jesus is the fulfilment of Old Testament prophecy and second because the literary form of the gospels is not that of myth. Like Papias, Justin classifies the gospels as ἀπομνημονεύματα. He may well be comparing them with the *Apomnēmoneumata of Socrates* by Xenophon, since he uses this work (though without mentioning its title) in his *Second Apology*, and frequently compares Jesus with Socrates.[2] The gospels are ἀπομνημονεύματα which come from the apostles.[3] More precisely, they can be described as "composed by the apostles and by those who followed them".[4] Here Justin is probably relying on the preface to Luke, where we find the same word for "follow" and a similar word for "compose" (Luke 1.1,3). Scholars have sometimes thought that he is referring to two gospels by apostles (Matthew, John) and two by followers (Mark, Luke). But soon afterwards he refers to a statement found only in Mark 3.16–17 and ascribes it to the *Apomnēmoneumata of Peter*.[5] It looks as if he was not concerned with any careful distinction between apostolic and sub-apostolic gospels. Indeed, to refer Mark's gospel to Peter means to emphasize its ultimate apostolic origin and to treat its authority as equal to that of either Matthew or John.

We should add that while Justin almost certainly knew the fourth gospel he rarely made use of it, and he never cites passages from it as derived from ἀπομνημονεύματα. It may be that at Rome the synoptic gospels were regarded more highly than John was. We know that at a later date at least one Roman Christian explicitly rejected the fourth gospel.[6] And the words of Jesus found in it can hardly be classified as "brief and concise".

Were these gospels inspired by the Spirit or Logos of God? Justin does not say so. But he does say that though the twelve apostles were unlearned and unable to speak (with any rhetorical skill) they were imbued with power from God which enabled them

---

[1] *Apol* 1, 54, 2.   [2] *Apol.* 2, 11, 2–7.   [3] *Apol.* 1, 66, 3; *Dial.* 100–7.
[4] *Dial.* 103, 8.   [5] *Dial.* 106, 3.   [6] See p. 28 below.

to proclaim the gospel.[1] Presumably this divine power, present in their oral preaching and teaching, was reflected in the work of those who compiled their words.

Justin's main concern, however, was not with divine inspiration but with historical accuracy. He believed that non-Christian readers could find evidence for the gospel story of Jesus' birth in tax declarations submitted under the procurator Quirinius and (*ex hypothesi?*) available at Rome a century and a half later.[2] Similarly he instructed his readers to look in the Acts of Pilate for confirmation of the miracles of Jesus and details about his crucifixion.[3] Presumably such official documents did exist, but it is not certain whether Justin has them in mind or is thinking of the Christian forgeries we encounter later.[4]

What Justin does not mention is also worth noting. While he believes that Jesus was born in a cave, he does not say that the cave is available for inspection; Origen, writing a century later, is the first to say so.[5] Again, while he thinks that as a carpenter Jesus made ploughs and yokes—presumably because they are mentioned in Luke 9.62 and Matt. 11.30—he does not say that they have been preserved.[6] Justin was not concerned with the later trend toward confirming New Testament statements by archaeology.

The four canonical gospels were not the only sources of information for the life of Jesus which Christians possessed in the first half of the second century. The oral tradition, from which these gospels had been compiled, continued to flourish, as we can see from the statement of Papias. And Papias himself, according to both Irenaeus and Eusebius, recorded in his writings some oral traditions which are not found in the gospels. Moreover, there were various apocryphal gospels, some circulated under the names of apostles supposedly responsible for their contents, others named

---

[1] *Apol.* 1, 39, 3. This statement implies the inspiration of the "gospel", however, not that of the written gospels (cf. 1.33,5).

[2] *Apol.* 1, 34, 2; for the translation cf. Kübler in *RE* IV A, 1899.

[3] *Apol.* 1, 48, 3; 35, 9.

[4] Cf. J. Quasten, *Patrology* I (Westminster, Md., 1950), pp. 115–18.

[5] *Dial.* 78, 5; Origen, *C* 1, 51, p. 102.

[6] *Dial.* 88, 8; cf. Irenaeus, *Adv. haer.* 4, 34, 4, p. 272. Origen (*C* 6, 36, p. 106) says that Jesus was not a carpenter.

for the groups of Christians who made use of them. The first class is represented by gospels ascribed to Peter and to Thomas, among others; the second includes the gospels "according to the Hebrews" (Jewish Christians) and "according to the Egyptians".

With his enthusiasm for oral tradition, Papias was willing to make use of a story of a woman "accused of many sins before the Lord"; and according to Eusebius this story was also to be found in the gospel according to the Hebrews.[1] It is by no means certain that Papias derived it from this book, but his preservation of it shows clearly that he did not confine himself to materials found in the four gospels. Indeed, his remarks about some of the gospels suggest that he was not very fond of them. They left out traditions which he thought ought to be retained.

Not only did Papias accept such traditions, but also Justin, who relied chiefly on the four gospels, made use of traditions not derived from them. It is likely that most, if not all, of these additional materials are derived from lost gospels.[2] Nevertheless, in Justin's time a reaction was evidently setting in against the use of materials not found in the four gospels. The four were regarded as authoritative by most Christians; the other gospels were not.

The most significant attempt during the second century to recover the life of Jesus was that made by a certain Tatian, trained in grammar and rhetoric according to his own testimony, and at one time a disciple of Justin at Rome. Tatian clearly built upon the results achieved by his predecessors in analysing the nature of the gospels. Papias had pointed out that the gospel of Mark was not written in order, and Tatian rarely followed Mark's order where it was not paralleled by that of Matthew. Papias had followed John's order in providing a list of the apostles, and Tatian, as we shall see, came close to the same sequence. Moreover Tatian's conception of the gospels as historical documents is very much like that set forth by both Papias and Justin. He differs from his predecessors however, because he probably did not make use of any material not found in the four canonical books.

[1] Eusebius, *H.E.* 3, 39, 17.
[2] Cf. E. R. Buckley in *JTS* 36 (1935), pp. 173–6.

No one knows precisely where or when Tatian compiled his *Diatessaron*, a synthesis of the four canonical gospels. The earliest references to it are found in the Syriac *Doctrine of Addai* and in Eusebius, but Irenaeus, Clement, and Origen make no mention of the work.[1] On the other hand, at Dura Carl Kraeling discovered a Greek fragment of the *Diatessaron* which comes from the early third century.[2] It was in existence even though ecclesiastical writers maintained silence about it.

To-day the *Diatessaron* is lost, as far as its original text is concerned; but its framework can be recovered from a group of late witnesses whose evidence is available in a treatise published by J. H. Hill in 1894. Hill relied almost exclusively on an Arabic version of a Syriac *Diatessaron*. His conclusion that this version probably represents the original arrangement of Tatian's work is still generally, and rightly, maintained by scholars.[3]

At first glance the *Diatessaron* resembles a patch-work, or more precisely a "crazy-quilt". After taking blocks of verses from John, Matthew, and Luke, Tatian began his real work of weaving together at a point where Marcan materials became available; and from that point onward his arrangement necessarily began to deviate from that provided by any one of the four gospels. One might suppose, since he begins and ends with verses from the fourth gospel, that the Johannine order was that which he favoured. This is not the case, however. At some points he corrects the synoptics by John, but more often he corrects John by the synoptics. Thus he follows the Johannine order from the beginning to the end of the first sign of Cana (John 2.11). But he transfers the cleansing of the temple (2.13–22) to Jesus' last visits to Jerusalem because the synoptic evangelists place it there. He removes from this point a comment on "signs" worked by Jesus (2.23–5), since only one has been performed. And he places Jesus' conversation with Nicodemus (3.1–21) in

---

[1] Eusebius, *H.E.* 4, 29. Both Clement and Origen knew the *Oration* of Tatian.

[2] C. H. Kraeling, *A Greek Fragment of Tatian's Diatessaron from Dura* (London, 1934).

[3] J. H. Hill, *The Earliest Life of Christ* (Edinburgh, 1894); cf. E. Preuschen and A. Pott, *Tatian's Diatessaron aus dem arabischen übersetzt* (Heidelberg, 1926); A. J. B. Higgins in *JTS* 45 (1944), pp. 187–99; B. M. Metzger in *JBL* 69 (1950), pp. 261–80.

Jerusalem because it refers back to "signs" (3.2) and because elsewhere (8.50; 19.39) Nicodemus is found only in Jerusalem. Similarly the discourse with the Samaritan woman (4.4–45a) is moved to a later point in Jesus' ministry because the synoptic outline does not allow for a journey through Samaria at this stage. The healing of a paralytic at Jerusalem and the discourse based on it (5.1–47) are set later because the witness of John the Baptist is regarded as past in the account (5.33–5).

Tatian feels free to rearrange the twelfth chapter of John. His own sequence is as follows: a plot against Lazarus (12.9–11), the anointing of Jesus (12.3–8), a comment by the evangelist (12.16),[1] the triumphal entry (12.12–15, 17–18), the discourse related to the Greeks (12.19–36a), Jesus' final words about judgement (12.42–50), and the evangelist's summary (12.36b–41). It is evident that he regards the twelfth chapter as something rather artificially constructed by John. Its order is not chronological. And doubtless he reaches this conclusion not only by comparing John with the synoptics but also by observing the extent to which the evangelist has provided editorial comments.[2]

On the other hand, though he places the cleansing of the temple late he separates it from the triumphal entry, presumably because John does so, although the synoptic evangelists do not. And from John 13.1 (the beginning of the farewell discourses) to the end of the gospel Tatian is able to preserve the Johannine order, with one insignificant exception (19.19–22 follows 19.23–4). Indeed, he uses the Johannine passion narrative as the foundation of his own and correlates the synoptic accounts with it.

John, then, provides Tatian not with history—except for the passion narrative—but with materials for a history. What of the synoptic gospels? In recording the narrative of the birth and infancy of Jesus, as we have said, Tatian alternates blocks of material, not easily reconcilable, derived from Matthew and Luke. When these gospels begin to agree, since their order comes to be the same as that of Mark, he follows the common sequence. He

---

[1] The comment, originally applied to the entry as a whole, is now referred to the fulfilment of the prophecy of Zechariah.

[2] Tatian feels free to make transfers of synoptic summaries as well.

refrains, however, from using Matt. 4.12–16 (Mark 1.14) or Luke 3.19–20 at the beginning of Jesus' ministry. His reason for placing them later is that they state or imply that the ministry began after John's imprisonment. Tatian follows the gospel of John, which places the beginning of the ministry before that event (cf. 4.24). In other words, when he is confronted with a choice between statements explicitly historical-chronological in nature, he follows John against the synoptics. Usually he does not have to make choices of this sort.

Most of the time, in describing the ministry of Jesus, Tatian follows the order of Matthew. He pays absolutely no attention to Luke's arrangement of Jesus' teaching within the framework of a journey to Jerusalem (Luke 9.51—18.14). Indeed, the passage with which Luke introduces this peripatetic teaching (9.51–56) is removed from its context and placed after the cleansing of the temple, just before the triumphal entry. As for Mark, Tatian follows him chiefly where he agrees with Matthew.

Sometimes he follows sequences already established by Mark or Luke and thus diverges from the Matthaean order. Sometimes he follows sequences found in none of the three. For instance, at the end of a Matthaean collection of teachings (Matt. 11.1) he places the story of Martha and Mary (Luke 10.38–42) which illustrates these teachings, and adds a Marcan summary (Mark 6.12 13) and a word about the imprisoned Baptist from Matt. 11.12–19. Presumably he found these passages as difficult to locate as we do.

Sometimes he arranges his materials by subjects. For example, on riches and wages (following a Johannine discourse, John 7.2–31) he provides the parable of the rich fool (Luke 12.13–21); the story of the "rich young ruler" synthesized from Matt. 19.16–30, Mark 10.17–31, and Luke 18.18–30; the parable of the rich man and Lazarus (Luke 16.14–27); the parable of the labourers in the vineyard (Matt. 20.1–16); and two parables about banquets from Luke 14.1–24 (the second combined with Matt. 22.1–14).

The conclusion we should draw from this analysis of his methods is that he believed that Matthew provided the most reliable historical account of the ministry of Jesus before the passion,[1] while John's passion narrative was the most trustworthy of the four. Mark's order is accurate in so far as it corresponds with that of Matthew. But Luke's arrangements of the teaching of Jesus possess almost no historical validity whatever.

Tatian's admiration for Matthew did not require him to follow him all the time. For instance, where Matthew has the sermon on the mount (5.1), Tatian follows Luke 6.17 in placing it on level ground. Presumably he feels that Luke has corrected Matthew for the sake of historical accuracy. And as we have already seen, he does not hesitate to separate the cleansing of the temple from the triumphal entry, or to correct Matthew's Marcan notion that Jesus' ministry began after the arrest of John the Baptist.[2]

This means that in Tatian's view the evangelists cannot have been inspired in such a way that they were provided with absolutely accurate historical–chronological information about Jesus. He omits Luke 1.1–5, where the evangelist speaks of his intention to write accurate history. Of this omission Hill says that "the preface of St. Luke, dealing with his private reasons for writing a Gospel, was scarcely suitable for Tatian's work".[3] More than that: Luke indicated that his purpose was exactly the same as Tatian's; and since Tatian so often rejects the constructions of his predecessor he could hardly retain the passage. Indeed, in Tatian's opinion all the evangelists were subject to error. Though he made an effort to preserve every scrap of information they provided, he cannot have held the theory that their memories were infallible.

It was Tatian's intention to provide a way by which the seeming discrepancies in the four gospels could be reconciled. In place of the four, he wished to create a single gospel, based on the approved methods of historical research and going beyond the prejudices of the individual evangelists to the one true portrait of Jesus which they inadequately represented. His method

---

[1] Hence Matthew's call (Matt. 9.9) is placed early. The order in which the apostles were called (Andrew, Simon, Philip, Nathanael, James, John, Matthew) thus resembles that intimated by Papias.

[2] He thus gives the sequence Matt. 4.17–22 (Mark 1.15–20); Luke 4.14–22[a]; 5.1–11; John 3.22–4, 3[a]; Matt. 4.12 (Mark 1.14).

[3] Op. cit., p. 25.

was ultimately historical in character. Where the evangelists were in general agreement, he followed all four; where they disagreed, he gave the account which seemed most probable to him. In assessing probabilities he undoubtedly relied on the tradition of the priority of the apostolic Matthew to the sub-apostolic Mark and Luke, and he treated John as an apostolic writer who arranged his gospel for symbolical purposes. He felt free to provide a different arrangement from John's but he evidently believed that John did not invent symbolical narratives. John must have been using facts symbolically.

In other words, Tatian was an historian and was not concerned with philosophy or even with philosophical rhetoric. Questions of credibility lie completely outside the range of his interest. He was concerned not with what the evangelists may have meant but with what they reported. And like Papias and Justin he has no doctrine of the evangelists' infallibility or about a hidden meaning they intended to convey. Or rather—since such a conception of hidden meaning does appear in his Oration to the Greeks—no doctrine of this sort is intimated in the *Diatessaron*.[1]

We should suggest that Tatian viewed the gospels as Justin had viewed them. They were ἀπομνημονεύματα, memoranda which represented a point halfway between their sources in oral tradition and a finished product which could be regarded as the work of a competent historian. In Tatian's opinion he himself was such a competent historian, one who took the materials unfinished by others and worked them into a synthetic whole.

We thus reach a view of Tatian which makes him not unlike more modern critics of the gospels who have abandoned the outlines of the ministry of Jesus provided by the evangelists and have tried to create outlines of their own. The chief difference between him and his successors lies in their refusal to take the fourth gospel seriously, though in very recent times we can find signs of a return to his position. And his rearrangement of the gospels verse by verse, or sometimes phrase by phrase, suggests a comparison with the work of some critics of the fourth gospel.

The question of the adequacy of this method, however, still

[1] On Tatian and rhetorical methods cf. *HTR* 51 (1958), pp. 123–8.

remains. Without a foundation in a strange doctrine of verbal inspiration—verbal but non-contextual—it is hard to see how the method can be justified. And it is difficult to believe that a doctrine of inspiration which pays attention to syllables, so to speak, and neglects the sequences intended by the evangelists is a doctrine of inspiration at all. The real upshot of Tatian's method seems to be that the evangelists wrote neither scripture nor history.

The *Diatessaron* represents a radical effort to solve the problem created by the disagreement of the evangelists. But it was not a book which appealed to most Christians, and the difficulties in it both theological and historical finally led to its condemnation by leaders of the Church.

Continuing use of literary and historical criticism of the gospels can be seen in the debate related to Montanism, a debate in which the fourth gospel was especially important. The latter half of the second century saw the rise of the Montanist movement in Phrygia and the claim of its leaders that the coming of the Paraclete, prophesied in the gospel of John, had been fulfilled in the advent of their prophet Montanus. Against this claim Christians in Asia Minor, later joined by an influential Roman presbyter named Gaius, argued that the fourth gospel should not be accepted because of its disagreements with the synoptic gospels.[1]

According to Epiphanius, they quoted Johannine verses from John 1.1—2.1 in order to contrast them with the outline provided by the other evangelists, who "say that Jesus spent forty days in the wilderness, tempted by the devil, and that then he returned and received his disciples".[2] Again, Mark "nowhere speaks of the birth from above[3] but says, 'In the Jordan the Spirit came down upon him, and there was a voice which said, This is the beloved Son, in whom I am well pleased.' "[4] And while John mentions two Passovers (2.13; 6.4), the other gospels mention only one.[5]

In other words, for these Christians the synoptic gospels provided the historical norm for an account of the life of Jesus.

---

[1] Cf. A. Jülicher in Pauly-Wissowa, *RE* VII, pp. 509–10. [2] *Haer.* 51, 4, 10.
[3] John 3.3,7 combined with 1.14. [4] *Haer.* 51, 6, 14. [5] Ibid., 51, 22, 1.

The gospel of John had to be rejected since it contradicted the synoptic account, especially on matters of chronology.

We know that Roman writers like Gaius were deeply concerned with the factuality of the Christian tradition. It was he who, in response to Asian claims probably related to John, told the Montanists that Roman Christians could point to the "trophies" of Peter and Paul.[1] The *aedicula* found under St Peter's is almost certainly one of the monuments he had in mind.[2] In his view, the search for fact meant maintaining the concrete reality of Peter and Paul and rejecting the unhistorical gospel of John. Gaius' rejection evoked an elaborate reply—now lost—from Hippolytus of Rome, and exercised considerable influence on the thought of Origen.[3] Two things were wrong with Gaius' attack on the Johannine literature. First, he wrote too late. At the time he criticized the Johannine books they had become firmly established in the life and thought of the Churches and could not be rejected from the canon in process of formation. Second, he assumed that the synoptic tradition was absolutely reliable as contrasted with the fourth gospel. Such an assumption could not have been justified by the simple comparisons he provided.

We might imagine that more light on Johannine–synoptic contradictions would be shed by those who wrote on the controversy over the celebration of Easter. This controversy arose because some Christians celebrated the Passover with Jews and others criticized them for doing so.[4] The divergence could be important in relation to the gospels, since the synoptics apparently regard the last supper as a Passover meal, while John indicates that the supper took place before the Passover.

Melito of Sardis was a Quartadeciman; that is, he advocated celebrating the Passover on the fourteenth (*quartadecima*) day of the Jewish month Nisan. But a fragment allegedly derived from his writings suggests that he combined the gospel of John with the synoptics.[5] According to this fragment, the "two natures"

[1] Eusebius, *H.E.* 2, 25, 6–7.
[2] J. Toynbee and J. W. Perkins, *The Shrine of St Peter* (New York, 1957).
[3] Cf. A. d'Alès, *La théologie de saint Hippolyte* (Paris, 1906), pp. xlvii–l.
[4] B. Lohse, *Das Passahfest der Quartadecimaner* (Gütersloh, 1953), pp. 50–89.
[5] Migne, *PG* 89, col. 229; Otto, *Corp. Apol.* IX, pp. 415–16.

of Christ are reflected in the gospels—his deity by the signs worked in the three years after his baptism (John 2.13; 6.4; 11.55), his humanity in the thirty years before it (Luke 3.23). If this fragment were indubitably genuine, as it is not, we should find not only a synthesis of the gospels but something like the later analysis of their differences. John emphasizes divinity; the synoptics emphasize humanity. But this doctrine seems to originate with Origen.

Apollinaris of Hierapolis wrote against the Quartadecimans. He said that his opponents relied on Matthew to show that Jesus ate the paschal lamb with his disciples on the fourteenth Nisan and suffered on the next day. "According to them the gospels seem to disagree."[1] Apollinaris' own principal authority must have been the gospel of John, to which he plainly alludes in a fragment from one of his writings. But since in his view the gospels did not disagree, he must have believed that they could be synthesized. Perhaps he held that John was the historical authority on this question and that the other gospels were to be interpreted in its light. In this way no disagreement would result.[2] We shall presently see that this procedure was followed by Clement of Alexandria.

The Unity of the Gospels

We find, then, that in the last quarter of the second century several leaders of Christian Churches were insisting upon the unity of the four gospels and their inspired authors. Theophilus, Bishop of Antioch, speaks of the unanimous teaching of "the holy scriptures and all the Spirit-inspired men, one of whom, John," wrote John 1.1–3. He provides collections of biblical passages to demonstrate the unity between the teaching of the prophets and that of "the gospel voice" or "the gospel". And he describes the Holy Spirit as "teaching and reminding" the Old Testament prophets, thus using a phrase derived from John 14.26.[3]

From this period comes the famous Muratorian fragment, of

[1] PG 92, col. 80–1; Otto, Corp. Apol. IX, pp. 486–7.
[2] Lohse, op. cit., pp. 136–7.   [3] Ad Autolycum 2, 22. 3, 13. 3, 14. 3, 11.

doubtful provenance.[1] Its beginning is lost, and what we have starts with the words, *Quibus tamen interfuit et ita posuit,* "with whom (which?) he was present and thus wrote them down". Presumably the words refer to Mark, and to Mark's having been a companion not only of Peter but also of Paul and Barnabas. The fragment may be defending Mark from the charge that his gospel is not the work of an eyewitness, and that its order is wrong. *Tertium evangelii librum secundum Lucam,* "the third book of the gospel is that according to Luke". Like Mark, Luke "did not see the Lord in the flesh", but after the ascension he was a companion of Paul and wrote his gospel in his own name. Evidently for the author of the fragment both Mark and Luke are inferior to the gospels written by apostles. And the gospel of John seems to be the most valuable of the four. Encouraged by his fellow-disciples and bishops, John urged them to fast with him for three days and to tell one another whatever would be revealed to each of them. Revelation immediately came to the apostle Andrew; all were to give their assent, but John was to write down everything in his own name. This legend is presumably based on John 21.24, a mysterious statement about the evangelist, whose testimony "we" know is true.

The author of the fragment is obviously concerned with the historical, or rather legendary, details he is reporting. But he is even more concerned with the unity of the gospels. Because of the unanimity of the testimony to the authenticity of John's gospel, he can say that "therefore", while different beginnings (*principia,* probably an allusion to the contradictions in the opening chapters of the gospels) are taught in the various books of the gospels, there is no difference for the faith of believers. All the gospels are inspired by the Spirit. All have Jesus' nativity, his passion, his resurrection, his life with the disciples, and his double advent— first in humility, second with royal power.

Here we find a leap of faith which is not clearly related to reason. The details about the evangelists in the first part of the fragment do not prepare us to see how the contradictions make

[1] Cf. H. Koch in *ZNW* 25 (1926), pp. 154–60; J. Quasten, *Patrology* II (Westminster, Md., 1953), pp. 207–10.

no difference. No evidence is provided for the inspiration of the gospels beyond the legend about the fourth evangelist. And the list of the contents of the four gospels hardly does justice to what we actually find in them.

There was room for a more adequate analysis, and an attempt to provide it is what we find in the treatise *Adversus Haereses* by Irenaeus, Bishop of Lyons. Irenaeus was strongly convinced of the necessity for the unity of the Church, which in his mind was related to the unity of God, the unity of revelation, and the unity of the scriptures. He found such unity delineated in the book of Acts, which he used extensively in his writings. But he was aware that not everyone accepted Acts (the Muratorian fragment defends the book as containing the acts of all the apostles in one volume). And therefore he had to provide historical evidence of its reliability. Luke was present at most of the events he describes, says Irenaeus, because (1) there are "we-passages" in the book; (2) in describing Paul's journey to Rome he records precise data about persons, places, and times; and (3) he was with Paul at Rome because he is mentioned in 2 Tim. 4.10–11 and in Col. 4.14.[1] Moreover, if one compares Gal. 2 ("after three years . . . after fourteen years") with the book of Acts, one finds that the chronology is the same, and therefore the same apostolic council is described in both; this proves that the apostles were all in agreement.[2] One might suppose that Paul's letter contradicts such a pleasant picture, but Irenaeus' text of Gal. 2.5 read "we yielded in subjection for a time", not "we did not yield".[3] Paul has thus become a symbol of unity rather than the historical protagonist of gentile freedom whom we meet in some of his letters.

Since we find Irenaeus concerned with historical questions in dealing with Acts, we are not surprised to find the same concern exhibited in his treatment of the gospels. He knew Papias' treatise on the Dominical Oracles, and it may well be that his information is derived from this work. In any case, he is convinced that the information he has is correct. Matthew was the

---

[1] *Adv. haer* 3, 14, 1, pp. 74–5, Harvey.
[2] Ibid., 3, 13, 13, pp. 74; 3, 12, 13, pp. 69–71.   [3] Ibid., 3, 13, 13, p. 74.

first to write, at a time when Peter and Paul were still preaching the gospel at Rome. He composed his gospel among the Hebrews in their language. After the "exodus" of Peter and Paul (probably their deaths, as in 2 Pet. 1.15), Mark, Peter's disciple and inter-preter, wrote down what Peter preached. Around the same time, Luke, the follower of Paul, wrote the gospel preached by the apostle. At a later date (*epeita*), John, the Lord's disciple who reclined on his bosom, wrote his gospel in Ephesus in Asia Minor.[1] The chronological sequence of the gospels is thus established as Matthew—Mark—Luke—John, though the relative priority of Mark to Luke is a matter of indifference, as Irenaeus soon makes clear.

He goes on to indicate something of the theological signifi-cance of the work of the various evangelists, though he is obviously considering only the opening chapters of their works. The three synoptists show that the story of Jesus fulfilled Old Testament prophecy; this can be proved from Matthew's story of the Magi, Luke's infancy narrative as a whole, and Mark's beginning with quotations from the prophets. John's purpose was different: he wrote against the Jewish-Christian heretic Cerinthus and spoke of the generation of the Logos.[2]

Finally Irenaeus starts over again, this time following an order based on that of the apocalyptic figures in Rev. 4.7. John wrote of the generation of the Logos; Luke emphasized Jesus' sacerdotal rôle; Matthew spoke of him as a human being; and Mark stressed the importance of prophecy. This sequence also has meaning in relation to the history of salvation in the Old Testament. The Logos or Word appeared to the Old Testament patriarchs; priestly office was given in the Mosaic law; the Word came to the Old Testament prophets; and finally the Word became man for us. It is evident that here we have passed far beyond history to a mystical-typological theory. If Irenaeus is still thinking about the sequence in which the gospels were written, he must mean that it implied a reversal of the order of revelation in the Old Testament. But we do not know that he has this sequence any longer in mind. History has been swallowed up in speculation, as it has when

[1] Ibid., 3, 1, 1, pp. 3–6.   [2] Ibid., 3, 9–11, pp. 32–44.

Irenaeus tells us that there are four and only four gospels because there are four winds, four corners of the earth, and so forth.[1]

When Irenaeus deals with gospel chronology his mind turns to fantasy. The Valentinians held that Jesus' ministry lasted one year. They were wrong, for according to John, the Lord's disciple (John 8.56–7), Jesus was "not yet fifty years old". Since Jesus must have passed through all the stages of human development from infancy to old age, he was forty-nine years old at the time, and later reached fifty. But Luke 3.23 says that Jesus was about thirty years old, and Luke 3.1 refers to the fifteenth year of Tiberius. Therefore, if Jesus' ministry lasted for twenty years, Pontius Pilate must have been procurator of Judaea not under Tiberius but under his successor Claudius (41–54)—and so Irenaeus states in his later *Demonstration of the Apostolic Preaching*.[2] He does not say how he thinks this notion can be reconciled with the chronology of Paul's life. He must not have considered the question.

In his discussion of the gospel of Luke, important because distorted critically by Marcionites and exegetically by Valentinians, Irenaeus begins with the analysis of Acts which we have already mentioned. He then points out that Luke is the only source of information for many important features of the life and teaching of Jesus. First, there are passages in the first three chapters of Luke which are rejected by Marcion but allegorized by the Valentinians; second, there are sayings of Jesus which are accepted by Marcion and the Valentinians alike. His basic point is obviously that the heretics do not agree and that therefore the whole gospel ought to be accepted.[3] It should be noted that among the passages accepted by Marcion are Luke 17.5–6 (which Harnack wrongly called "un-attested")[4] and Luke 13.6–9 (which Epiphanius said Marcion deleted).[5] Because of Irenaeus' testimony both passages should be regarded as parts of Marcion's gospel.

This is a significant example of detailed literary criticism. Irenaeus evidently compared Luke with the other gospels and

[1] Ibid., 3, 11, 8, pp. 48–9.
[2] Ibid., 2, 22, 5, pp. 331–2; *Dem.* 74.   [3] Ibid., 3, 14, 3–4, pp. 76–8.
[4] Harnack, op cit., 223*.   [5] Ibid., 217*.

Marcion's version with the orthodox one. We may infer that his description of Marcion's gospel as omitting everything about the Lord's generation, as well as many of his sayings,[1] is probably based on comparative study, not on hearsay. We should conclude that Irenaeus, like other early Christian writers, was more competent in literary criticism than in historical analysis. He does not seem to be able to tell the difference between his rather sensible analysis of the authorship of Acts and his discussion of the Lord's age and the date of the crucifixion, and for this reason he cannot be regarded as a witness to the existence of historical study in the Christianity of his time.

CLEMENT OF ALEXANDRIA

At the end of the second century there were thus several solutions available for the problem presented by the four gospels. The field of investigation had been narrowed by the rejection, among most Christians, of any gospels not among the four, and the general insistence that no fewer than the four were to be used. But how were the four to be used? And how was the problem presented by their disagreements to be solved? In other words, what use was to be made of each in getting back to the life of Jesus?

It is in the writings of Clement of Alexandria that we find the beginnings of an attempt to synthesize information previously available. From "tradition"—more probably older learned conjecture—he knows that the gospels with genealogies (Matthew, Luke) were the first to be written.[2] He adds the detail that Matthew's diet consisted of seeds, leaves, and vegetables, with no meat.[3] In regard to Luke he reports the conjecture that he translated the epistle to the Hebrews from Hebrew, since its Greek style is the same as his.[4] It is hard to tell which of the two gospels Clement thought was written first. We should expect him to favour Matthew, but in discussing the sermon on the mount he says that Matthew "added" "in spirit" to the beatitude

---

[1] Irenaeus, *Adv. haer.* 1, 27, 2, p. 217.   [2] Eusebius, *H.E.* 6, 14, 5.

[3] *Paed.* 2, 16, 1. Could this be based on the fact that Matt. 3.4 reports the diet of John the Baptist, while Luke does not?

[4] Eusebius, *H.E.* 6, 14, 2. Actually they are not the same.

about the poor, and "for God's righteousness" to that concerning those who hunger and thirst.[1] Probably he has in view as a source the words of Jesus common to both Matthew and Luke.

What he says the elders told him about Mark looks like a garbled version of the report of Papias.[2]

> In Rome Peter preached the word and, inspired by the Spirit, proclaimed the gospel. Since Mark had followed Peter for a long time and remembered what had been said, many persons asked him to write down what was said. He did so, and delivered the gospel to those who had asked him. Peter knew of this gospel, but by way of recommending it neither discouraged nor encouraged the work.

This comment restricts the inspiration of Mark to the materials he derived from the inspired Peter. The composition of the gospel was at best neutral in character. In other words, among the elders whom Clement knew there was no unbounded enthusiasm for the work.

On the other hand, both Clement and the elders admired the gospel of John and undertook to explain why it differed from the synoptics. Its differences were both chronological and literary, as well as theological.

> Last of all John, aware that the "corporeal facts" (τα σωματικα) had been made plain in the ⟨previous⟩ gospels, and encouraged by his companions, and inspired by the Spirit, created a spiritual gospel.

What Clement says about the time, the circumstances, and the inspiration of the fourth gospel closely resembles what we have already found in the Muratorian fragment. What is new, however, is his idea that the gospel deals not so much with factual information as with spiritual meaning. Clement himself was devoted to allegorical exegesis,[3] and by treating John's gospel as primarily allegorical he believed that he could explain the difference between it and the synoptics.

Indeed, he may have held that it gave the true, post-resurrection "gnosis" delivered by Jesus to his disciples. This gnosis, says Clement, was given to Peter, James, and John; from them it passed to the other disciples and thence to the seventy.[4] Now

[1] *Quis dives salvetur?* 17, 4.   [2] Eusebius, *H.E.* 6, 14, 6–7.
[3] Cf. W. den Boer, *De Allegorese in het werk van Clemens Alexandrinus* (Leiden, 1940).
[4] Eusebius, *H.E.* 2, 1, 4.

since Peter did not write a gospel and did not commend that of Mark, and since James did not write a gospel, the gnosis must be contained in only one of the four gospels—that of John.

Of course Clement does not deny that John has any factual information. When he deals with the vexing question of the Last Supper, he argues that what Matthew calls the preparation for the Passover (26.17) was on the thirteenth of the month Nisan, and that this was the time of the footwashing in John 13.[1] "Our Saviour suffered on the following day"—i.e., the fourteenth of Nisan. This, he says, agrees with John 18.28, according to which the Passover meal is still future. "All the scriptures agree and the gospels are in concord." By relying on John as a historical document he has been able to refute the Quartadeciman arguments.[2]

Clement thus treats the synoptic gospels as histories (of varying quality) and the fourth gospel as a mixture of historical fact and spiritual truth. But since in spite of his concern for the religious history of mankind, to which Mondésert has drawn attention,[3] he is not really concerned with historical fact, we do not find in his writings any genuine feeling for the historical difficulties which still remain even when John is viewed symbolically. Such a feeling we encounter only in the writings of Origen.

Moreover, Clement insisted that the synoptic gospels, like that of John, contain symbols as well as history. This point becomes clear in his homily, *Who is the Rich Man who is Saved?* (a title itself based on allegory). Here he quotes Mark 10.17–31 in full, adding that the same general sense is found in the other accepted gospels. His basic concern is with the principle that "the Saviour teaches his people nothing in a merely human way, but everything by a divine and mystical wisdom". Therefore "we must not understand his words literally but with due inquiry and intelligence we must search out and master their hidden meaning".[4] Matthew is a witness to this mastery, as is shown by the additions we have already mentioned.

[1] The same sequence is found in Tatian (Matt. 26.14–17; John 13.1–20).
[2] Fragment *de Pascha*; Stählin III, pp. 216–17.
[3] C. Mondésert, *Clément d'Alexandrie* (Paris, 1944,) pp. 187–219.
[4] *Quis div. salv.?* 4–5.

GREEK LITERARY AND HISTORICAL CRITICISM

BEFORE we turn to examine the contribution which Origen made to the study of the gospels, it is time to say something about the methods which both he and his predecessors employed. We sometimes think that textual, literary, and historical criticism were created in the eighteenth and nineteenth centuries, or that at any rate they were not previously applied to the gospels. By this convenient fiction we can present ourselves with a picture of early Christianity in which we can see faith constantly triumphing over intelligence—a picture attractive, for different reasons, both to the very orthodox and to the very unorthodox.

Such an image, either of the ancient world in general or of ancient Christianity in particular, is thoroughly distorted. We have already seen methods of literary criticism and historical analysis being employed by such Christian writers as Papias, Justin, and Irenaeus; we know that these authors did not invent the methods they used; and we possess enough information about the work of textual, literary, and historical critics in the Graeco-Roman schools so that we can say something about the procedures they followed. In addition, we possess introductory manuals for the study of rhetoric, coming from the late first century and the early second, which enable us to obtain a fairly clear picture of what the educated Greek or Roman was taught in school. He learned how to analyse literary compositions with a rigour certainly unparalleled in modern education. And the methods he learned did not slip from his memory if he became a Christian.

We need say very little about textual criticism, for on the one hand it was not discussed in the manuals of rhetoricians and, on the other, it was not especially significant in Origen's work on the gospels. First, the work of ancient textual critics was almost entirely subjective; this is the case, for example, in their work on the *Odyssey*;[1] it is also the case in the work of such Christian writers as Marcion, Julius Africanus, and Origen himself. Second, while Origen knew how textual errors originated—he ascribes them to simple mistakes in copying, to misplaced ingenuity in emendation, and to theological bias[2]—his own practice is extremely unsatisfactory. He can discuss textual variants at considerable length,[3] or suggest the presence of interpolations;[4] but I can recall only one passage where he removes such an interpolation (Matt. 4.17: "repent"), and there his judgement is certainly wrong.[5]

LITERARY AND HISTORICAL CRITICISM: THEON

We are often tempted, as I have said, to suppose that ancient writers were incapable of undertaking the task of historical criticism. This temptation should be avoided, since they actually did undertake it. The proof comes not only from Graeco-Roman historians and from treatises like that of Lucian *On the writing of History*, but also from manuals of rhetoric in which the approved method of analysis was set forth, sometimes for students, sometimes for teachers. These manuals show not only that the method existed but also that it was taught in the schools.

The study of rhetoric as a science had been revived in the second century B.C. and although rhetoricians had often contended with philosophers for the prize of students' attention, by the first century of our era there were many who recognized the usefulness of philosophical conceptions and made use of them in their systems, though without adhering to any one philosophy. And while some rhetoricians kept alive the conflict between those who considered rhetoric an art and those who regarded it as a

---

[1] M. van der Valk, *Textual Criticism of the Odyssey* (Leiden, 1949).

[2] *M* 15, 14, pp. 387–8.

[3] Ibid. also *M* fr. 194, p. 93; *C* 1, 62, p. 113; cf. J.–P. Audet, *La Didaché* (Paris, 1958), pp. 63–7; pp. 420–1. On Romans 16.25–7 Origen discusses the readings of Marcion's text and of other witnesses but makes no attempt to explain them (*Rom. comm.*, *PG* 14, 1290A–B).

[4] *J* 32, 20, p. 462; *J* 32, 32, p. 479; *M* 134, p. 274 (but cf. Cant. II, p. 140; L fr. 83, pp. 273–4; *C* 2, 33, p. 159).

[5] *M* fr. 74, p. 45. Cf. Hanson, *Allegory and Event*, pp. 176–7.

science, most of them were prepared to go ahead without the benefit of a definition.

The point at which definition was important was that at which the various literary forms were differentiated. Thus for Theodore of Gadara in the first century B.C. the careful definition of historical narrative was obviously significant. "Narrative is the setting forth of an action, complete in itself, with mere statement, about things which have already happened."[1] The sole virtue of this form (i.e., that for which the narrator should aim) is "probability" or "persuasiveness" (πιθανότης).[2] Later writers criticized Theodore for his excessive technicality, but he thought that every word in his definitions was necessary. We shall meet the word "mere" again in Origen.

When we mention "probability" we have to consider criteria of probability, and the rhetoricians were also concerned with this problem. The student of rhetoric was expected to be able to apply the methods of ἀνασκευή (refutation) and κατασκευή (confirmation) to myths, narratives in general, brief sententious sayings, and laws.[3] We find these methods discussed in the *Institutio oratoria* of Quintilian and in the *Progymnasmata* of the Alexandrian Aelius Theon, who as Lana has shown was probably one of Quintilian's principal sources.[4]

Theon's list of the points to be discussed in providing refutations is practically the same when he considers various literary forms, but the number of points (τόποι) varies. Thus in dealing with myths he gives eleven points (76.19–22), for narratives ten (93.14–32), for sayings nine (104.15–18), and for laws eight (129.8–10). In the second century Hermogenes was able to reduce the list to six items.[5]

[1] Anonymous Seg., I, 434, 25 Spengel; W. Stegemann in *RE* V A, 1853.

[2] Ibid., 440, 1.

[3] This order is that of the manuscripts, though cross-references show that it is not the original one (Stegemann in *RE* V A, 2042).

[4] I. Lana, *Quintiliano, il "Sublime" e gli "Esercizi Preparatori" di Elio Teone (Università di Torino, Pubbl. della Facoltà di lettere e filosofia* III, 4, 1951), pp. 110–51. On Theon's Stoic education, ibid., pp. 110–13; Stegemann in *RE* V A, 2049–50. Text in L. Spengel, *Rhetores Graeci*, II, pp. 57–130.

[5] Hermogenes, *Progymnasmata*, p. 9, 4–7 Spengel (11, 8–10 Rabe, Leipzig, 1913). In Hermogenes' view ἀνασκευή could not be applied to myths since they are absolutely false (8, 31 Spengel, 11, 4 Rabe).

The most complete analysis is thus that provided for myths, and we shall examine it while adding something of what Theon says on historical narratives. Since by Theon's definition a myth is "a false account portraying truth" (λόγος ψευδὴς εἰκονίζων ἀλήθειαν, 70.21; 72.28), he does not need to show that it is impossible (76.6); on the other hand, in dealing with narratives regarded as historical, he has to show that the events could not have taken place at all or that they could not have taken place at the time mentioned by the historian (93.18). Some say, Theon points out, that Heracles killed Bousiris; but according to Hesiod Bousiris lived eleven generations before Heracles (93.20).

Both myth and history can be criticized because of their obscurity, which arises either out of the matters being described or the diction used in describing them (76.22; 80.8). For instance, the subject matter of Thucydides is unclear because he presents various events in relation to summers and winters, and therefore has to keep going back and forth when he describes a single sequence of related events (80.15). "A narrative becomes obscure because of the omission of what it was necessary to mention, and because of the 'allegory' of the matters concealed" (81.4).

He can also show that either a myth or an historical narrative is incredible. "The incredible (ἀπίθανον) is something which can take place or be said, but is not believed to have taken place or to have been said" (76.32). Such an analysis does not rest upon mere assertion. It rests upon a detailed analysis of a story in relation to the person to whom the action or saying is referred; the place in which it is said to have happened; the time; the mode; and the reason assigned to the action (77.1–9).[1]

Theon gives an example of a story regarded as historical, and proceeds to show why it is incredible; this is the account of how Medea killed her children (94.12–32). The person, a mother, would not have harmed her children. The action itself is incredible, since she would not have slain them. She would not have done so in the place (Corinth) where their father Jason was living.

[1] Cf. also 77.12 and 94.10.

She would not have done so at the time when she had been humiliated and Jason possessed greater power than she did because he had married the king's daughter. The mode of action is an unlikely one; she would have tried to conceal her action, and since she was a sorceress she would have used not a sword but a poison. Finally, the reason assigned to her action is most improbable. Anger against her husband would not have driven her to kill the children who were hers as well as his; she harmed herself as well as him, and indeed she harmed herself more, since women are subject to emotion more than men are.

In the same way, he can show that a story is inappropriate (77.9)—though it is hard to see what the difference between the incredible and the inappropriate is, especially in view of the example Theon has provided.

He can also show that a myth or a narrative suffers from the omission of necessary information or the addition of irrelevant information about persons, actions, times, modes, places, reasons, etc. (77.10).

Then he can proceed to show that there is some disagreement with history as generally accepted or with suppositions generally held. For example, the writer may be saying that men were formed not by Prometheus but by some other god, or that the ass is intelligent and the fox is stupid (77.14). Such unusual statements would have to be rejected.

Perhaps the writer contradicts himself; perhaps he does not use the right sequence in telling his story. He may omit necessary information at the beginning, or he may fail to end the story as he should (77.18-23). The order of the chapters may be wrong (93.29). Again, he may be led astray by the prejudicial tone of his writing (77.27).

Finally, the conclusions or "morals" drawn from a myth may be wrong. They may not really be related to the story which has just been told. They may be false. "Those who desire more are deprived of what they have" is false, since it is not universally true (77.29—78.3).

Not all these topics are always relevant in dealing with historical narratives, says Theon (93.12). But the student of rhetoric should discuss them in the order set forth in the manual. "If we should suppose that the action is possible, we must say that it is incredible; if it turns out to be credible, we shall see whether it is false; if it should appear to be true, we shall go on to ask if there is some deficiency or redundance; next, that the author himself contradicts the narrative; in addition, we shall criticize the order of the chapters . . ." (93.24-30).

The method which rhetoricians had developed for the analysis both of myths and of historical narratives possessed several merits. It was logical; it could be understood easily; and it could be employed rather simply and straightforwardly. Unfortunately, its shortcomings were even more striking. Concentrating its emphasis on logical matters, it left no room for the operation of non-rational factors in historical events. And— perhaps the most important drawback—it was used in an effort to classify narratives as either true or false. In the conclusions there was room for either black or white, but no room for the grey tones in which much historical writing is painted. All that one could find in history consisted, on the one hand, of true history, an accurate record of real events, and, on the other hand, of fiction (what could have taken place but did not) and myth (what could not have taken place). The schematized logical analysis of the record, in short, resulted in a schematized logical conclusion.

Moreover, precisely the example which Theon used—the story of Medea's killing her children—was subject to other kinds of analysis which the rhetoricians did not employ. Writers who were concerned with understanding the human psyche recognized that in Medea there was an irrational power stronger than reason; though she knew that what she was about to do was evil, she proceeded to do it. And since she did it, an analysis of the event in relation to nothing but rational-prudential categories is ultimately meaningless.

This is to say that while some aspects of the rhetorical method are right—a single event cannot have taken place at two different places or on two different occasions, given the actuality of space and time—much of it involves applying purely external considerations which may well not be relevant. Since so much of the method depends on the analysis of psychological factors, it is a pity that the rhetoricians' psychology was so inadequate.

DIO AND OTHERS

Early in the second century the method of ἀνασκευή was applied to the Iliad by the rhetorician Dio Chrysostom. In his eleventh oration, *Troica*, he uses it in an effort to prove that the Trojan war never took place. And as W. Kroll pointed out, the oration follows the lines laid down for the ἀνασκευή;[1] indeed it could be regarded as an exercise in the method.

Dio begins by criticizing human credulity, which he ascribes to a desire for notoriety. Men prefer hearing slander about their ancestors to not hearing about them at all. Truth deserves defence, however, and Dio will provide a refutation of Homer's false statements, relying only on his own poetry.[2] The first thing he mentions is not actually from Homer's poems but from Homeric tradition. Homer is said to have been a beggar. If this is so, he is not likely to have been especially trustworthy. Moreover, the character of his poetry confirms one's doubts. His hero Odysseus told lies, and Homeric statements about the gods, as nearly everyone agrees, are not to be taken literally. Indeed, the conversations which the gods are supposed to have held often took place without any witnesses present. Perhaps Homer was not concerned with such a problem; but in the *Odyssey* Odysseus tells how he learned about the gods' debates from Calypso, and how she had heard about them from someone else. The problem therefore is a real one. It is not made less acute when Homer pretends that the gods have a language all their own and that he understands it.[3]

The basic difficulty with the story of Troy, however, is posed by the way in which Homer wrote it. He begins haphazardly, not with the proper beginning; he does not bring the story to an end. The real origin of the war was the abduction of Helen, and he describes this in such a way as to make it psychologically and historically incredible. The real end was the capture of Troy,

---

[1] *Rheinisches Museum* 70 (1915), 607–10; on the method in general, *RE* Suppl. VII, 1119.
[2] *Or.* 11, 1–11.   [3] Ibid., 15–23.

which he does not describe at all.[1] Many details and episodes in what Homer does relate are false, and the story of Patroclus and his death is simply a distortion of what must actually have happened to Achilles.[2]

Dio does not keep his promise to disprove Homer solely from Homer. Following a Hellenistic literary fashion, he introduces an aged Egyptian priest who knows the true story of Troy because it was told in Egypt by Menelaus and preserved in temple archives.[3] But this is simply a literary device; the priest uses the kinds of arguments employed by Dio himself. The basic substance of the oration is provided by the ἀνασκευή.

Later on, as we have said, Hermogenes simplified the method by reducing the number of categories to six. In his *Progymnasmata* he gives examples of each. An example of obscurity is the time when Narcissus lived; of improbability, that Arion would want to sing while in difficulties;[4] of impossibility, that Arion would be saved on a dolphin; of the inconsequent and inconsistent, to save the state and to wish to destroy it; of the unsuitable, for Apollo a god to have intercourse with a mortal woman; of the prejudicial, "when we say that it is by no means expedient to hear these things" (11.10).

G. Reichel tells us that such manuals as that of Theon were forgotten because they were used more by teachers than by their pupils, and because the method advocated by Theon was too complicated.[5] But what actually seems to have happened is that the textbook material sprovided by Theon were simply absorbed into other textbooks. Such a process does not lack modern analogies. And as we shall see the complexity of the method did not deter writers who liked complexity from using it.

For example, in the later rhetorical manual of Aphthonius we see a method like that of Hermogenes being applied to a myth, a story of something which could not have taken place.[6]

---

[1] Ibid., 26–30.   [2] Ibid., 97–102.   [3] Ibid., 37–8.
[4] Cf. Theon, p. 93, 23 (an allusion to the story).
[5] *Quaestiones progymnasmaticae* (Leipzig, 1909), p. 46. In Hermogenes' curriculum more advanced students learned to deal with details about place, time, mode, person, reason, and action (*De inventione*, II 212–18 Spengel; 140–8 Rabe).
[6] II, 28–30 Spengel.

Aphthonius first sets forth the story of Daphne, daughter of the earth and the river Ladon, who, pursued by Apollo, was received back by the earth; a laurel sprang up in her stead. Then he proceeds to criticize lack of clarity, impossibility, unsuitability, inconsequence, and inconsistency. (1) How could Daphne have known that she came from the earth and a river? How could the earth and a river be united in marriage or bring forth a human being? (2) By whom was the infant fed? (3) How did a god love, and by desire betray his nature? (4) Why could Apollo not succeed in catching Daphne? Why did her mother help her avoid marriage, since marriage is good? And finally the story is inconsistent. Earth encouraged Apollo by bringing forth Daphne, but then she grieved him by rescuing the girl from him. On these grounds (which seem to overlap a good deal) Aphthonius has shown that the story is a myth. He has already criticized those who told it by pointing out their contradictions. "It is irrational for the poets to deny that they are eager to contradict one another when they first make up these stories about the gods. How then is it not irrational that none of the gods made an account for them but that we have the poets' account?"

In other words, the method of ἀνασκευή can involve criticism of both the theological content and the literary forms encountered in dealing with myths. And in Aphthonius' manual, the only result of κατασκευή, defence of the story, is a thorough going allegorization. First one can speak of the reputation of those who told the story—the poets, inspired by the Muses. Then one can say that (as an allegory) the story is perfectly clear, for all things are born from water and earth. It is quite possible, provided one remembers that virtues are acquired only by effort. It is consequent, since all mortals return to the earth. It is suitable, since the earth does receive men and does bring forth trees. And it is expedient or fitting, since Daphne is really Sophrosyne, temperance.[1]

From the passages we can see how closely related were grammatical-rhetorical criticism of stories on historical grounds and the use of the allegorical method in their defence. Many of the

[1] Ibid., 30–2.

ingredients with which a theologian like Origen was to be concerned are already present in the rhetorical manuals, including even the question of the inspiration of authors who contradict one another. And we shall later see that in dealing with the gospel stories he uses the method taught by the manuals.

As an example of the concern for the authenticity of religious literature in this period we may take the problem which arose in relation to Orphic literature. Did the very ancient seer Orpheus write the literature ascribed to him? Long before, Herodotus had said that Onomacritus of Athens had edited and published the oracles of Orpheus' disciple Musaeus; and a fourth-century Athenian historian had stated that Orpheus himself could not have written anything, for he was a Thracian and therefore illiterate.[1] In the second century of our era there was a great deal of theorizing about the work of Onomacritus. He collected, revised, and interpolated the Delphic oracles; he wrote the Orphic poems, or most of them; he wrote the oracles ascribed to Musaeus. Greek witnesses to this kind of analysis include Plutarch, Pausanias, and Sextus Empiricus; the Christian rhetoricians Tatian and Clement of Alexandria simply reproduce what had already been said.[2]

The analogy between the Orphic literature and the gospels is obvious. If Orpheus could not have written because he was illiterate, a similar claim could be made about the gospel writers, since according to the Christian tradition none of the apostles could write. The gap between oral tradition and written gospels was therefore bridged by means of a theory of inspiration such as Justin probably provided; Origen, as we shall see, certainly did so.

POSSIBLE ALTERNATIVES

We should not suppose that everyone accepted the rhetoricians' rules without question. Sextus Empiricus devotes a chapter to an attack on the grammarians who, like rhetoricians, claimed to be

[1] Androtion cited by Aelian (early third century after Christ), *Var. hist.* 8, 6.

[2] Plutarch, *De pyth. orac.* 25, 407b; Pausanias and Sextus Empiricus in I. M. Linforth, *The Arts of Orpheus* (Berkeley, Calif., 1941), pp. 350–3; Tatian, *Or.* 41, p. 42. 4 Schwartz; Clement, *Str.* 1, 131, 1, cf. 3.

able to analyse history by classifying it as factual, false, and like the truth.[1] Actually, says Sextus, there is no "scientific and general consideration" which would make it possible to deal with history in this way. "There is no technical knowledge either of things infinite or of things which vary from hour to hour. But particular histories are both infinite, because of their great number, and without fixity, because the same facts are not recorded by all respecting the same person."[2] It is all very well to classify history as real history, myth, and fiction, or to say that "though the subject-matter of history lacks method, yet the judging of it will be a matter of art". The trouble with this kind of analysis is that there is no criterion of true history, and there is no rule as to how history should rightly be written.[3] Therefore historical analysis is really impossible. As Sextus says when he discusses poetry, in distinguishing true and false statements "what is useful is not grammar but that which is capable of making the distinction, namely philosophy".[4] This kind of claim is, of course, characteristic of philosophers. Rhetoricians simply ignored it.

It is obvious that the discussions we have mentioned are concerned with what German writers call *Sachkritik*, analysis of the content of a narrative supposed to be historically true. In antiquity there was very little employment of *Quellenkritik*, analysis of the sources which narrators had used. There was considerable discussion of forgery and plagiarism,[5] but it was usually carried on in order to discredit one's opponents or predecessors. One of the rare statements to be found about sources occurs in Arrian's preface to his account of the expedition of Alexander the Great.

> Whenever Ptolemy son of Lagus and Aristobulus son of Aristobulus give an identical account, I follow this with complete confidence in its accuracy. Where they disagree, I choose the version which, in my judgment, is the more credible and at the same time the more interesting of the two.

These grounds of judgement are not as objective as one might

[1] *Adv. math.* 1, 248–69.   [2] Ibid., 259–60.   [3] Ibid., 267–8.
[4] Ibid., 280.   [5] Cf. K. Ziegler in *RE* XVIII 1, 1956–97.

wish. But Arrian goes on to explain why his sources deserve respect. Both writers were companions of Alexander, and Ptolemy was a king; both wrote after Alexander's death and therefore did not need to misrepresent the facts.

This kind of analysis was completely neglected by the Christian writers who, under the spell of *Sachkritik*, dealt with the gospels. Their emphasis on inspiration, valuable as it was, prevented them from asking how the evangelists knew what they wrote about.

3

ORIGEN AND THE GOSPELS

THE MOST important Christian critic in antiquity was Origen of
Alexandria, born about 185 and brought up in a Christian home
where Greek education was highly valued. At an early age he
worked at both the Christian scriptures and the Greek "encyclical
studies" such as grammar, rhetoric, geometry, and arithmetic.[1]
His studies were directed not only in a Greek school but also at
home, where his father Leonidas "advanced him in secular subjects".[2] It is probable that he also studied, perhaps a little later,
with the Christian teachers Pantaenus and Clement; at any rate,
Alexander of Jerusalem says that he became acquainted with
Origen through these teachers,[3] even though Origen himself
never mentions having been taught by either. After his father's
martyrdom in 202, the family property was confiscated and
Origen taught grammar and rhetoric, as well as the study of
scripture, in the Christian catechetical school. Soon afterwards,
when he was appointed dean, he sold his library of secular
literature for an annuity of 4 obols a day. As A. S. Pease points
out, Eusebius does not say to whom he sold it,[4] and it may well
have remained available for his use. He continued to teach the
encyclical subjects, and later did "graduate work" with the philosopher Ammonius Saccas.[5] By the year 217 he had decided to
concentrate his attention on biblical and theological studies, and
his pupil Heraclas took over the encyclical work.

This brief sketch of Origen's education and early life shows
that until he was about thirty years old he was constantly engaged
in the kind of rhetorical studies we discussed in the preceding
chapter, and that rhetorical interpretation of literature had to be
an important part of his exegetical method. The goal of his exegesis was the spiritual meaning. Its starting point was, and

---

[1] Eusebius, *H.E.* 6, 2, 7–8; 6, 18, 3.   [2] Ibid., 6, 2, 15.   [3] Ibid., 6, 14, 9.
[4] Ibid., 6, 3, 9; Pease in conversation 26 August 1958. The expression "four obols"
was proverbial for any small amount (cf. Clement, *Quis div. salv.?* 21, 5; Aristaenetus
Ep. 2, 16, p. 167 Hercher).   [5] Ibid., 6, 19, 12–14.

50

remained, historical-literal analysis. Both Cadiou and Klostermann have shown that school definitions are employed in his
writings both early and late.[1]

His critic Porphyry laments his exodus from secular studies
but insists that he was "always with" Plato, Numenius, Cronius,
Apollophanes, Longinus, Moderatus, Nicomachus, and other
Pythagorean writers, and that he used the books of the Stoic
Chaeremon and Cornutus. How did Porphyry know? Bidez is
undoubtedly right in suggesting that he had seen Origen's library
at Caesarea.[2]

What did these authors contribute? Origen undoubtedly used
Platonic theology in the development of his own. Most of the
other writers gave him insights into the relation between theology
and literature. For example, Cornutus could have shown him
how to separate ancient tradition from mythological interpolations (though this is not Origen's method);[3] Cronius insisted
that inconsistency in the *Odyssey* indicated the need for allegorical
exegesis.[4] Numenius himself interpreted the Old Testament
allegorically,[5] and Moderatus was an important first-century
teacher of number symbolism.[6] The only point at which Porphyry seems to have been quite wrong is in his mention of
Longinus; this rhetorician-philosopher was certainly Porphyry's
teacher, but hardly Origen's, since he was probably born when
Origen was about thirty.[7] We can perhaps save Porphyry's word
by taking it as a symbol of Origen's concern for rhetoric, not in
relation to style but as a method of analysis.

We learn something more of Origen's interests from the
panegyric addressed to him in 238 by Gregory Thaumaturgus
after five years of study with him at Caesarea. From this oration
it is quite clear that Origen taught a philological method. He was
not concerned with analysing vocabulary and style, but he did
provide a scientific background in "physiology" (the study of

---

[1] R. Cadiou, *La jeunesse d'Origène* (Paris, 1935), p. 28; E. Klostermann in *ZNW* 37
(1938), pp. 54–61.
[2] *Vie de Porphyre* (Ghent, 1913), 13; Eusebius, *H.E.* 6, 19, 8.
[3] *The Letter and the Spirit*, pp 21–2.
[4] Test. 9 Leemans, pp. 155–6; cf. *JTS* N.S. 10 (1959), p. 155.
[5] Test. 17 Leemans, p. 87=Origen, *C* 4, 51, p. 324.
[6] Cf. W. Capelle in *RE* XV, 2318–20.   [7] Aulitsky in *RE* XIII, 1401–15.

nature), geometry, and astronomy. This was useful for the study of scripture.[1] Since from Origen's commentaries we know that he was actually concerned with the biblical vocabulary we must assume that Gregory did not share this interest and therefore refrains from mentioning it.

Origen not only taught but wrote. Beginning about the year 215 he composed treatises such as that *On the Resurrection*, the *Stromateis*, and the great catechetical-theological work *De principiis*. These works show that exegetical problems were already important to him, and around the same time he began his commentaries on the first twenty-five psalms, on Lamentations, and on the beginning chapters of Genesis. Before he left Alexandria in 231 he had completed five books of his first New Testament commentary, that on the gospel of John, and perhaps some of his homilies on Luke.

After he was ordained priest at Caesarea he was removed from the catechetical school by Demetrius, Bishop of Alexandria, and expelled from the city. Thereafter he taught at Caesarea, with occasional visits elsewhere before his death about 253. There he composed the last twenty-seven books on John, apparently over a considerable period of time, as well as the rest of his homilies on Luke and his treatise *On Prayer*, much of which is devoted to exegesis of the Lord's Prayer. Between 244 and 249 he wrote the *Commentary on Matthew*. Since he ascribed no special significance to Mark he did not provide separate exegesis for this gospel. Finally, around 248 he composed his eight books *Contra Celsum*, an answer to an anti-Christian treatise written seventy years earlier.[2]

THE FOUR EVANGELISTS

What Origen tells us about the four evangelists comes to him partly from tradition and partly from his own detailed studies of their works. By "tradition" we mean the older information based sometimes on fact, sometimes on conjecture, and handed down

[1] *Pan.* 106–13; cf. 182. It is worth noting that the word "allegory" does not appear in this oration, though we find both *ainigma* (174, 180) and *kataskeuasma* (168) twice. For Origen's use of lexicographical works cf. R. Cadiou in *Revue des études grecques* 45 (1932), pp. 271–85; the citations from Origen are from works both early and late.

[2] For details about Origen's commentaries and homilies see Appendix.

without much, if any, investigation of its sources. Occasionally Origen modifies tradition or, at least, chooses between two alternative traditions. For example, before his time at Alexandria Clement had taught that the gospels were written in the order Matthew-Luke-Mark-John; Origen returns to the view, set forth by Irenaeus, that the sequence was Matthew-Mark-Luke-John.[1] In other words, while in Clement's view Luke preceded Mark, in that of Irenaeus and Origen Luke wrote after Mark. Does this conclusion have any historical or theological significance? No, it does not. Origen, like Irenaeus, is not interested in source-analysis. Indeed, he explicitly denies that Luke made use of any of the other canonical gospels when he wrote. One might conceivably suppose that the preface to Luke contains an implicit criticism of Matthew and Mark. But Origen rejects such a supposition. When Luke says (1.1) that previous writers "undertook" to compose an account of the life of Jesus, he must be referring to authors of apocryphal gospels. They are the ones who composed "rashly and without a gift of grace". None of the Church's four evangelists "undertook" to write anything; all were inspired by the Holy Spirit.[2] Origen's theory of inspiration excludes source-analysis.

His emphasis on the inspiration of the evangelists is the most striking feature of what he tells us about them. Probably observation rather than inspiration was responsible for their exact knowledge of Judaean geography.[3] But it is certain that Origen viewed the evangelists in much the same way as he viewed the apostles. "In them there was no power of speaking or of giving an orderly narrative by the standards of Greek dialectical or rhetorical arts." The apostles did not know even the rudiments of grammar.[4] But according to tradition two gospels were written by these men, two by their immediate followers. Given the reliability of the tradition, how could the gospels have been written at all? Origen's answer to this question is that their authors were inspired by the Holy Spirit. The Spirit taught them grammar and composition. In other words, their writings are the

---

[1] Eusebius, *H.E.* 6, 25, 4–6.
[2] *L* 1, p. 4. [3] *J* 6, 41, p. 150. [4] *C* 1, 62, pp. 113–14; cf. Acts 4.13.

result of the Spirit's work both in content and in form. No purely literary or historical explanation of their work is either necessary or possible.

Moreover, since their work was directed by the Spirit it cannot contain errors. At three different points in Origen's commentaries he explicitly states that inspiration implies freedom from error. (1) Some may suggest that the evangelists' narratives differ from one another because their memories were inaccurate; Origen denies that this is the case. (2) Critics of the gospels may suggest that they are "not true and not written by a more divine Spirit or recorded in orderly fashion, for the gospels are said to have been composed in various ways". Origen rejects this view. (3) His own opinion is this: "we believe that the gospels were accurately written by the aid of the Holy Spirit, and those who wrote them made no mistakes in recording".[1]

We have translated the Greek word ἀπομνημονεύειν in two of these passages by the English "record" even though it can also mean "remember" because it appears that Origen's primary emphasis is laid upon the written compositions involved rather than upon a pre-literary process. In this regard we may compare what he says about the epistle to the Hebrews, which in his view was not written by the apostle Paul. He states that the thoughts are the apostle's (hence, are divinely inspired) but the style and composition are the product of one who recorded (or remembered) the apostle's teachings and, as it were, made short notes on what his master said. Here it looks as if his emphasis lies not on the disciple's memory but on the recording of the master's words; the note-taking is simply a more precise description of the recording.[2] It is not clear whether the note-taking was the product of inspiration or not. In the case of the evangelists, however, their similar procedure was inspired.

Because of this emphasis on inspiration, Origen does not find the historical circumstances of the various evangelists especially meaningful. For example, in dealing with the evangelist Matthew he sometimes states that he had two names, Matthew and Levi, in accordance with Hebrew custom; but in the treatise *Contra*

[1] *J* 6, 34, p. 143; *J* 10, 3, p. 172; *M* 16, 12, p. 510.   [2] Eusebius, *H.E.* 6, 25, 11–14.

Celsum he says that Matthew and Levi were two different persons.[1] He knows something from tradition about Matthew's purpose in writing: he wrote for converts from Judaism, and in Hebrew.[2] Like the other synoptic evangelists, Matthew laid more emphasis on Jesus' humanity than on his divinity—though the importance of this emphasis can be exaggerated. Some suppose that the divinity is not stressed in his gospel, but according to Matt. 16.8 the Saviour can read men's thoughts; this is no merely human power.[3]

Origen raises but fails to solve one difficult problem in regard to Matthew's gospel. "Hosanna" in Matt. 21.9 makes sense neither in Hebrew nor in Greek, and Origen suggests that the word was added to the gospel by "Greek writers". Who could these Greek writers be? Harnack suggested that Origen meant the evangelist, but in Origen's view Matthew wrote in Hebrew. Klostermann claimed that he meant copyists of the gospel, and Origen certainly believed that copyists made mistakes.[4] We may tentatively suggest, however, that he meant those who translated the gospel from Hebrew into Greek, since it is a Hebrew word, not a Greek one, which is in question. If this suggestion is correct, a considerable difficulty arises in regard to the inspiration of the Greek text which we possess. Do we have an uninspired translation of an inspired document? Origen does not tell us. And while he does insist that the Greek translation of the Old Testament is inspired, he may not have been willing to say as much for that of the gospel of Matthew.

Of Mark Origen says very little; he only knows, following a tradition already criticized by Clement, that Mark was instructed to write by Peter and that Peter refers to his close relationship to Mark in 1 Pet. 5.13.[5]

Luke wrote an extremely accurate gospel. It is historically reliable, for Luke's opening words can be paraphrased as "I

---

[1] *L* fr. 7, p. 235; *R praef. PG* 14, 837*A*; *C* 1, 62, p. 113.
[2] Eusebius, *H.E.* 6, 25, 4; *J* 6, 32, p. 141.
[3] *J* 10, 8, p. 177; *M* 92, p. 210; *M* 126, p. 262; thoughts, *M* 12, 6, p. 77. The "some" may perhaps be Ebionites.
[4] Harnack in *Texte und Untersuchungen* 42, 4, 9; Klostermann, footnote ad loc., p. 542.
[5] Eusebius, *H.E.* 6, 25, 5.

3   55

write without accepting mere hearsay". On the other hand, it has a universal, non-historical quality. Some readers suppose that Luke wrote to a certain Theophilus, but actually all believers are θεοφίλοι, beloved of God, and therefore his gospel is not limited by historical particularity. Luke did not employ the expression "Father in the heavens" because he was not writing for Jews. Paul commends his gospel in 2 Cor. 8.18.[1]

Origen's favourite gospel is the fourth, that written by John, who reclined on the Lord's bosom. John emphasized the Lord's divinity; he preserved the "greater and more perfect words about Jesus"; he laid stress on the great works which Jesus did—works which were, however, more significant spiritually than literally. He was a theologian who used the Greek language with extreme care; this fact can be shown from his use of the definite article in reference to God the Father in John 17.3 and his omission of it in relation to the Son in John 1.1. He wrote for Greek readers and expected them to understand why he translated the name Thomas as "twin" in John 20.25.[2] Indeed, it is especially characteristic of John that he combines the seemingly historical with what has a deeper meaning (γυμναστικόν).[3]

One might suppose that this picture of John's work is contradicted by what Origen elsewhere says of it. In his view John, since he was "unskilled in speaking" (2 Cor. 11.6), expressed in a disjointed manner what he actually knew.[4] The seeming contradiction can probably be resolved, however, if one considers the fact that in Origen's view John possessed perfect knowledge, had been given the ability to write grammatically by the Holy Spirit, and wanted to use the common biblical method in recording revelation. This is to say that he wished to reveal some things plainly and to express other things obscurely so that men's minds would be directed toward deeper levels of reality. This purpose, given him by the Holy Spirit, coincided with his own lack of

---

[1] L 1, pp. 10–11; L fr. 42, p. 253; L 1, p. 6.

[2] John 13, 25; 21, 20; J 1, 4, p. 8; C 2, 73, p. 195; J 2, 2, p. 54; J fr. 106. pp. 516–2. The point about the definite article is ultimately derived from Philo, Somn. 1, 229.

[3] J fr. 74, p. 541; γυμναστικόν is dialectical rather than rhetorical. Thus John 4.6 is historical; John 4.10 is not.

[4] J 13, 54, p. 284.

ability to write clearly. Apparently Origen is trying to maintain both the complete inspiration of the sacred writings and the human characteristics of the sacred writers.

We have already seen that for Clement the fact that John wrote last of all had theological significance. A similar idea is expressed by Origen when he says that Christian preaching consists first of the "corporeal gospel", then of heavenly wisdom and the gospel of John.[1] From the synoptics he is aware that a certain process of development took place in the disciples' understanding of Jesus; at the beginning they did not understand the meaning of his mission (Matt. 16.20–1), and they first preached to Jews about Jesus, later about the Christ.[2] For the apostles came to be fully illuminated only after the resurrection, when they received the Holy Spirit.[3]

According to Origen a similar development took place in the life and thought of the apostle Paul, who gradually reached "a higher degree of perfection". By examining the Pauline epistles, Origen is able to place them in their chronological order. In Gal. 5.17 the flesh lusts against the spirit; in 1 Cor. 9.27 Paul still fears he may be rejected. But in 2 Cor. 4.8–10 he bears in his body the dying of Jesus; in Phil. 3.11–13 he is still imperfect but is reaching perfection; and in Rom. 8.35–9, nothing can separate him from the love of Christ.[4] Presumably Origen could have traced a similar process of development from Matthew to John, even though he does not explicitly do so. In any case, Origen certainly does not believe that the first gospel was the best.

We have observed what Origen did do and could have done with what information he had accumulated about the four evangelists. What he did is most conspicuous in his dealings with the differences between John and the synoptic gospels, which we

[1] *J* 1, 7, p. 13.   [2] *M* 12, 16, p. 106; 12, 17, pp. 107–8.

[3] *C* 2, 2, pp. 128–9. This process has its limits, however; it is "absurd" to suppose that men later than the apostles were "more blessed" than the apostles themselves (*J* 10, 43, p. 221).

[4] *Rom. comm.* praef., Migne, *PG* 14, 833–5. Since Romans was written from Corinth (835B–C), Philippians must have come from Ephesus. The crude eschatology of the Thessalonian epistles was presumably due to Sylvanus and Timothy, with whom, as Origen points out (1297D–99A), Paul wrote the letters. (In *C* 3, 20, p. 217, the order Ephesians-Colossians-Thessalonians-Philippians-Romans is not necessarily, though it may be, chronological.)

shall presently discuss in more detail. But it is equally important to notice what he did not do. The notion that Matthew wrote his gospel in Hebrew is presumably intended to explain why the atmosphere of the book is more Jewish than that of the other gospels. Origen, as we have seen, is acquainted with this notion; and we should expect him to make some use of it in explaining the differences between Matthew and the other gospels. He does not do so. For him, the notion is apparently no more than a miscellaneous datum of history, essentially meaningless and unusable. It is evident that although he insists upon the rationality of the evangelists' inspiration, this rationality does not have any relation to the historical circumstances under which it was operative. The rationality Origen has in view is essentially timeless and unhistorical. He never speaks of John as a philosopher, but he is willing to quote the first verse of his gospel as a statement of "our philosophy" about the Son of God;[1] and if this statement is philosophical, presumably the evangelist was concerned with philosophical thought. It would be better to say that the evangelist, though no philosopher, was an instrument of a philosophical revelation.

Could we expect Origen to have considered the evangelists' purposes more fully? We might think so if we look at his discussion of "personification" in *Contra Celsum*. Here he attacks Celsus for putting non-Christian statements in Christians' mouths, and he argues that consistency of character is important in a literary work. Homer is admired because "he keeps the character of the heroes the same as they were when he started, such as that of Nestor, or Odysseus, or Diomedes, or Agamemnon, or Telemachus, or Penelope, or one of the others".

On the other hand, "Euripides is made a fool of by Aristophanes for writing inappropriate verses, because he often attributed to barbarian women or slave girls words containing ideas which he had learnt from Anaxagoras or some other wise man". Origen's statement is hardly original; just the same contrast is pointed out by Theon.[2]

---

[1] *C* 5, 24, p. 25.
[2] *C* 7, 36, p. 187; Chadwick, op cit., p. 424 (cf. p. 245); Theon 60, 27.

We praise Homer for putting appropriate words into the mouth of each of his characters, but we find fault with Euripides because he unsuitably makes Hecuba discuss philosophy.

In other words, rhetoricians were well aware of the function of an author as creator of the personages in his story.

Origen does recognize this function to some extent when he notes the difference between John and the synoptic evangelists. He cannot develop the idea further, however, since for him there is really no middle ground between history and fiction or myth. To lay more stress on the creativity of the evangelists as historians would have meant that he could not pass so easily from literal truth or untruth to allegory. He would have had to abandon the rhetorical foundation of the allegorical method.

INSPIRATION AND CONTRADICTION

The anti-Christian writer Celsus took pleasure in pointing out the fact that the various gospels contradict one another. "Some believers", he said, "as though from a drinking bout, go so far as to oppose themselves and alter the original text of the gospel three or four times over, and they change its character to enable them to deny difficulties in the face of criticism."[1] As we have seen, Origen did not need to be informed by non-Christians that the gospels disagree with one another. The controversies of the previous century had made all intelligent Christians aware of the fact. In the face of it he was willing to employ the traditional answer that though there are four gospels they are really one,[2] but he was not willing to rest in the comfort provided by this declaration. His own critical studies, and probably his awareness of those made earlier by Gaius of Rome, made it necessary for him to try to analyse the contradictions as sharply and precisely as possible. His advice to the reader of his *Commentary on Matthew* reflects the procedure he followed.[3] "By placing the gospels side by side at these passages and comparing them, you will find out what is said." (In passing we may suggest that this sentence implies that the gospels were available on scrolls as well

[1] C 2, 27, p. 156, tr. H. Chadwick. Celsus may be using Marcionite arguments.
[2] J 5, 7, p. 104. [3] 16, 8, p. 490.

as in codex-form, for the work of comparison would surely be far easier for one working with scrolls than for one turning the leaves of a codex.) In any event, Origen firmly believed in the necessity of detailed critical comparison. He probably did not know the *Diatessaron* of Tatian, but if he knew it he did not accept it. Indeed, he brought difficulties to the attention of those who did not recognize their existence: he says that Celsus is probably unaware that in the gospels the genealogies of Jesus are inconsistent.[1]

In Origen's view some of the difficulties in the gospels were due to the way in which the text had been transmitted. In this process three kinds of errors could have been introduced: (1) those due to carelessness in copying; (2) those due to rashness in emendation of the text; and (3) those due to prejudiced correctors who made additions or deletions.[2] This last group of errors includes those intentionally made by enemies of the Church.[3] Origen says that his analysis has been confirmed by his experience in dealing with the variants to be found in the Greek Old Testament.

The particular passage with which he is dealing is that concerning Jesus' "counsel of perfection" (Matt. 19.19), where, as we have said, Matthew's sentence "Thou shalt love thy neighbour as thyself" is not found in either Mark (10.19) or Luke (18.20). Since Origen believes that Matthew was written first, he can argue that neither Mark nor Luke would have omitted the sentence had it actually been spoken by Jesus. And the extent of the textual variants in the gospels, he believes, justifies his treating it as a scribal addition.[4]

Not all, or even many, of the disagreements in the gospels can be accounted for on the basis of textual criticism. There are more serious difficulties, as Origen is aware, especially in regard to John and the synoptics. Indeed, says Origen, everything in the gospel story is a matter for controversy.[5] Christians say that Jesus had a virgin mother; Marcionites say he had no mother; Ebionites say he had a human father and mother. Some say his

[1] C 2, 32, p. 159.   [2] M 15, 14, pp. 387–8.   [3] M 134, p. 274.
[4] M 15, 14, p. 387.   [5] L 17, pp. 115–16.

body was from heaven; others say it was just like ours. After he rose, his body bore the marks of the nails, but it could pass through closed doors. Even the predictions of the prophets about him are subject to dispute.

The most striking differences, as earlier critics had pointed out, were to be found by comparing the sequences of events in the first few chapters of the synoptics and John. In the synoptics we find Jesus' baptism, his temptation in the wilderness, the beginning of his preaching in Galilee, and the call of his first disciples. In John we find the baptism, no temptation, the call of the first disciples, the first miracle at Cana, and the cleansing of the temple in Jerusalem (which the synoptists place toward the end of Jesus' ministry). Moreover, where the evangelists agree as to the sequence of events they describe the events somewhat differently. All this had already been pointed out by Gaius of Rome, and Tatian had tried to solve the difficulty by accepting the synoptists' order of events. But Origen was unwilling to agree that his favourite evangelist, "the most wise John", could have been wrong.[1]

Other people might suggest that the evangelists disagreed because the memories of some of them were inaccurate,[2] but in Origen's opinion, as we have seen, divine inspiration guaranteed correctness in remembering;[3] "none of the evangelists made an error or spoke falsely".[4] We may infer that this opinion of his was in part based upon his own phenomenal memory for scripture passages, clearly evident in his homilies and in his *Discussion with Heraclides and the other Bishops*, recently discovered on papyrus. If his own memory was so good, the memories of the inspired evangelists cannot have been less perfect. His opponents, he says, are really claiming that the gospels are not true, that they are not written by divine inspiration, that they are not recorded with a coherent arrangement.[5]

We shall presently discuss the way in which Origen endeavoured to solve the difficulties involved in these disagreements. Here, however, we wish simply to point out that some of

[1] J 10, 13, p. 183.   [2] J 6, 34, p. 143.   [3] M 16, 12, p. 510
[4] J 6, 34.   [5] J 10, 3, p. 172.

them arise from a confusion of inspiration with exact historical accuracy, as well as from an erroneous theory of the way in which the gospels were composed. It is possible that if Origen's own memory had not been so good he could have admitted that the evangelists were not always absolutely right. And had he been a less productive writer he might have seen that others sometimes copied from sources. In other words, his own genius stood in the way of his understanding the work of some, at least, of the evangelists.

When he himself copied from the writings of others, he usually did so either in order to use the documents as authorities (the Bible, Stoic definitions, etc.) or in order to refute them word by word (Heracleon, Celsus). The idea of taking a source and modifying it slightly (as in the case of Clement's use of Philo) was alien to him, and he was therefore unable to understand the method of the synoptic evangelists.

THE JOHANNINE-SYNOPTIC CONTRADICTIONS

Early Christian writers, as we have already seen, were well aware of the differences between John and the synoptic gospels; Hippolytus must have tried to explain them in his two works against Gaius. The importance of Origen's handling of the subject is due to his attempt to derive theological meaning from the differences. Analysis of the letter leads to insistence upon allegory.

Everyone was aware that John does not give a genealogy of Jesus or describe his temptation. How was this difference to be explained? Origen insists upon considering the purpose the fourth evangelist had in mind when he wrote. John began his gospel with God, and as a divine being Jesus had no genealogy. Moreover, John knew that God cannot be tempted; therefore he did not record the temptation.[1] That Jesus was tempted as a man is plain from Matt. 4.4: "Man shall not live by bread alone."[2] Here we seem to be on the edge of a neat explanation of this difference between the synoptics and John. The synoptics describe Jesus as a man; John describes him as God.

[1] L 29, p. 131; M 92, p. 210; 126, p, 262.
[2] P 3, 2, 1, pp. 245–6; L 29, p. 180.

The explanation is not really quite so neat, however, since Origen has already shown that the synoptic temptation narrative must be symbolical. In it we read that the devil took Jesus to a high mountain from which he saw the kingdoms of the whole world and their glory (Matt. 4.8; Luke 4.5). Only a "careless reader", says Origen, could imagine that with "the bodily eye" Jesus saw the kingdoms of Persia, Scythia, India, and Parthia.[1] The mode of action in the story is incredible, literally understood; therefore the story is an allegory. Origen therefore explains that the "kingdoms" must have meant a totality, i.e. the devil's rule over the whole world.[2] At another point he argues that it is "incredible" that the devil could have led or taken the Son of God anywhere; Jesus must have gone voluntarily, like an athlete going to a contest.[3] This argument is inconsistent with that by which he showed that the temptation story is an allegory, but we recall that it is used in a homily and that homilies sometimes express various aspects of a religious problem as treatises do not.

The basic point he has in mind is that the temptation story is primarily symbolical, whether it speaks of Jesus as a man or as the Son of God. Since both the synoptic gospels and that of John are dealing with symbols, they can be reconciled only by considering the symbols which lie behind their verbal expressions. The discord among the gospels is to be resolved by the use of allegorization (ἀναγωγή).[4]

An equally serious difficulty arises when we compare the place of the cleansing of the temple in John with that assigned it by the synoptic writers. Here there is a genuine "historical discord". And Origen proceeds to take the hypothetical case of four inspired writers—obviously the evangelists—who speak of God's presence "through an historical symbol". They will say that God appeared to a particular witness at a particular time in a particular place; that he performed a particular action, appeared in a particular form, and went away to another particular place. Since the writers are describing revelations given them individually, they will disagree. Literally understood, their accounts are false. They

---

[1] *P* 4, 3, 1, p. 324.   [2] *L* 30, pp. 184–5.   [3] *L* 31, p. 187.
[4] *J* 10, 3, p. 175.

are myths. They contain internal, not external, truth.[1] They can be recognized as myths because they disagree on just those points at which contemporary rhetoricians found myths and legends internally inconsistent. (See Chapter 2.)

Origen is now in a position to proceed to his criticism of the story of the cleansing of the temple. Taken as history, he says, the narrative is improbable (ἀπίθανος). The term he uses, as we have seen, is the one used by Greek analysts in criticizing narratives ordinarily regarded as historical. In his view the story of the cleansing of the temple not only is told differently by the various evangelists but also contains inherent improbabilities.[2] How could merchants have sold unclean animals in the temple? How could a person thought to be a carpenter's son have acted so boldly among "myriads" of people? To use a scourge of cords (supposing that someone prefers to refer the story to the Son of God rather than to Jesus) would hardly be characteristic of the Son. The story as told by John, then, is not literally historical.[3]

But the synoptic version is not historical either. Matthew cannot be writing history, for there is nothing worth recording in his statements about the two disciples who went to get an ass and a colt, or about Jesus' sitting upon them and entering the city.[4] If Matthew is writing for Jews and showing how prophecy was fulfilled, it is singular that the Jews themselves point out that the whole prophecy in Zechariah was not fulfilled. And as literal history his story is open to sharp criticism. A journey of fifteen stadia is hardly worth reporting. Again, how could Jesus ride on two animals at the same time?[5] And for the disciples to tell the ass's owner that "the Lord needs him" was unworthy of the Son of God.[6]

Once more, Origen's criticisms are not altogether consistent. Sometimes he speaks of what was suitable for the carpenter's son, sometimes of what the Son of God should have done or said. But they are intended to demolish the historicity of the narrative,

[1] J 10, 4, p. 174. [2] J 10, 22, p. 194.
[3] J 10, 25, pp. 197–8. [4] J 10, 26, pp. 198–9.
[5] Clement, *Protr.* 121, 1, had endeavoured to avoid the difficulty by stating that the two animals drew a chariot on which Jesus rode.
[6] J 10, 27, pp. 199–201.

one way or another, and details that could not be rejected as unworthy of Jesus could be rejected as unworthy of God's Son. The story must be taken symbolically. It is a story about the Logos, not about Jesus, and about the human soul, not about Jerusalem.[1]

Origen concludes, rather triumphantly, that there is "only one refuge" for those who wish to defend the story; this is the "more divine power of Jesus". By an appeal to this power they can support the historical character of the event—"if it took place".[2] But he has already pointed out that "when the four evangelists use many examples of deeds and words in relation to the marvellousness and paradoxical character of the power of Jesus, they have woven into the writing, describing it as perceptible to the senses, what was clear to them purely and through the mind alone".[3] This statement means that an appeal to the divine power of Jesus can be made only by a simple believer, not by a theologian.[4] For an Origenist will recognize that the work of "weaving in" is due to the divine author of scripture, who inspired the evangelists.

The way in which the weaving took place deserves a closer look. In Origen's systematic treatment of inspiration and exegesis he tells us that where spiritual truths did not correspond to historical events, "the scripture wove into the historical narrative what did not take place—at some points what cannot take place and at others what can take place but did not".[5] This is to say that scripture, like literature in general, contains a combination of various literary forms. Theon tells us that the well trained rhetorician will be able to create such combinations. He can combine one historical narrative with others (86.2; 92.24), or he can combine myth with historical narrative (74.3). For example, he can begin with a myth and can say that "a camel who wanted horns was deprived even of ears"; then he can state that "the experience of this camel seems to me to resemble what happened to Croesus the Lydian", and can go on to the narrative about

[1] *J* 10, 28, p. 201.　　[2] *J* 10, 25, pp. 197–8.　　[3] *J* 10, 5, p. 175.
[4] Cf. *L* fr. 15, p. 239 : simple believers are edified by considering the mighty works of God; others ought to go on to spiritual understanding.
[5] *P* 4, 2, 9, p. 322.

Croesus (75.9–16). Origen is pointing out that scripture is arranged in a similar fashion. It combines historical narrative with myth (what cannot take place) and fiction (what can take place but did not).

In his analysis of these forms, however, he does not use the prejudicial terms "myth" and "fiction". Instead, he substitutes the words "enigma" and "parable", since they are to be found in scripture itself. We know that these words are the equivalents of "myth" and "fiction" because Origen's definitions of them, provided in his *Commentary on Proverbs*, are identical with the Greek definitions of the ordinary Greek terms.[1] We might suppose that Origen's conception was different from that of the rhetoricians because he insists on the hidden meaning to be found in "enigma" and "parable", but the rhetoricians too claimed that "myth" contains an image of some truth.[2]

Under what circumstances did the evangelists, or the Logos or Spirit which inspired the evangelists, make use of enigmas and parables (to use Origen's terminology)? Origen says that usually the spiritual meaning and the literal expression of it coincide, but where spiritual truths cannot be expressed literally they are presented in symbolical form, indeed in what, literally considered, is practically false.[3] Once more his interpretation is close to what the rhetoricians said. "When will the orator speak falsely", asks Hermogenes, "if his audience is conscious that he speaks falsely?" The answer is that he will do so when the falsehood is of benefit to his hearers.[4] In other words, the rhetorician will make use of the beneficial or medicinal lie. According to Origen, God makes use of the same procedure, like a father dealing with an infant son or a physician treating a patient. "The whole of divine scripture is full of such medicines."[5]

At the time Origen wrote his tenth book on John he thus regarded the story of the cleansing of the temple as a medicinal

---

[1] E. Klostermann in *ZNW* 37 (1938), 58, 61, citing Lomatzsch 13, 220. 225–6. According to Tryphon (III, 193, 13) enigma includes something "impossible and impracticable".

[2] See the Glossary, p. 122.   [3] *J* 10, 5, p. 175.

[4] II, 441, 27 Spengel (435, 4 Rabe); cf. Sextus Empiricus, *Adv. math.* 7, 42–5.

[5] *Jerem. hom.* 20, 3, p. 180 Klostermann; cf. Hanson ,*Allegory and Event*, pp. 210–31.

myth. By using the method of ἀνασκευή he had shown that it was incredible. The place is wrongly described, for in the temple there were no unclean animals. The person, regarded either as the man Jesus or as the Son of God, would not have used a whip of cords; and therefore the mode of action is also incredible. The time ascribed to the action is improbable because there were so many people present. In addition, Origen had shown that the story was told inconsistently, since the Johannine version disagrees with that found in the synoptics.

To appeal to Jesus' miraculous power in defence of the story meant appealing to an authority to some extent outmoded. For Origen had pointed out that while the remarkable miracles were once able to evoke faith "they did not keep their impressive character with the passage of time, and are now supposed to be myths". This notion of the declining credibility of miracles is Stoic.[1] But who is the person who supposes them to be myths? It may be a non-Christian critic of the gospels. But it may also be, and in view of what we have said it probably is, Origen himself.

Origen certainly regretted having spoken so emphatically on this subject. By the time he wrote his thirteenth book on John he was ready to say that in dealing with the cleansing of the temple he had shown that Jesus was revealing his miraculous power—in spite of the fact that this is just what he had not shown.[2] Much later, in the *Commentary on Matthew*, he said that previously he had explained the Johannine narrative to the best of his ability; he had proved that the boldness and authority of one regarded as a carpenter's son was not inferior to the paradoxical miracles of the gospels. His allegorization of the narrative, he claims, was due to his "slavery to the letter".[3] Evidently his mind was changing.

But the extent to which it changed should not be exaggerated. In the same commentary Origen discusses the story of Jesus' anointing by a woman (Matt. 26.6–13; Mark 14.3–9; Luke 7.36–50; John 12.1–8).[4] Many, he says, suppose that the four evangelists are speaking of the same woman, and indeed there is a good

---

[1] *J* 2, 34, p. 92. Cf. Cicero, *De natura deorum*, 2, 5. Hanson, *Allegory and Event*, pp. 221–2.
[2] *J* 13, 56, p. 286.   [3] *M* 16, 20, pp. 543–4.   [4] *M* 77, pp. 178–86.

deal of material common to the four.[1] If one considers the details, however, it is clear that several women are involved. The ointment is poured on Jesus' head in Matthew and Mark but on his feet in Luke and John. In Luke she is a sinner, while in John she is Mary the sister of Martha; neither Matthew nor Mark calls her a sinner. In Luke she weeps, while in John she does not. In Matthew, Mark, and Luke the episode takes place in the house of a certain Simon, while in John it is in some other house. In Matthew the event occurs two days before the Passover, in John six days before it. In the synoptics nothing is said of the filling of the house with the odour of the ointment, as it is in John. Thus the stories contain descriptions of different circumstances, actions, places, times, and results, and on the grounds established in Greek rhetorical analysis, they are all incredible.

What conclusions can be drawn? Origen suggests three possibilities. (1) The evangelists may really contradict one another, and in this event some of them are speaking falsely. (2) They may be describing the actions of several women (but this possibility is excluded by the general resemblances in the stories). (3) "A little more boldly"—historically speaking, there were one, two, or even three women; but the main concern of the evangelists was with mysteries of faith, and they did not take sufficient pains (*non satis curaverunt*) to tell the story in accordance with the truth of history. Instead, they "wove in" spiritual truths—to which Origen turns.

It is obvious that in this passage, written late in his life, Origen was still adhering to the theory of "weaving in" which he had set forth in his treatise *De principiis* and had employed in the *Commentary on John*. His mind clearly did change in regard to the story of the cleansing of the temple, but it did not change so much that he abandoned his theory of the primacy of the spiritual. The truth of history remained secondary for him.

When he first dealt with the cleansing, Origen concluded that the only demonstrably historical items in the story were the existence of the temple itself and the presence of crowds at

---

[1] Tatian regarded the story as the same in Matthew, Mark, and John (39.7–17 Hill) but different in Luke (14.45—15.11).

festivals there. We may suspect that his notion of history is close to the content of Josephus's works, for in them we read of the temple and the crowds but not of Jesus' ministry.[1] In the story of the anointing, the historical items are the persons of Jesus and of one woman or more, and the act of anointing. Obviously there is a significant difference in Origen's treatment of the two stories, for in the exegesis we have just discussed he does not deny that Jesus was really present and was really anointed. Just as he has come to believe that there is more historical truth in the cleansing of the temple, so he finds that the anointing was a real event.

What is the meaning of Origen's change of mind, as far as his historical method is concerned? We are fortunate in possessing his exegesis of these two narratives which, in some respects, are remarkably similar. Both the cleansing and the anointing are placed near the beginning of the passion narrative by three of the evangelists but not by a fourth.[2] In both cases Origen feels that he must examine the details of the stories in order to find out what common elements they have and what differences are present. At points where differences exist, Origen claims in regard to both stories that spiritual truths have been "woven in". But in the story of the anointing, the weaving is confined to matters of detail. The principal reason for this difference seems to lie in Origen's diminishing confidence in the method of historical criticism set forth by the rhetoricians. By employing this method in order to assess the truth or falsity of the cleansing narrative he had reached the conclusion that it was literally, historically false. He could have used the same method in dealing with the story of the anointing, but he did not do so. Instead, he restricted himself to the comparison of the various accounts. Such a comparison led him to raise questions about various details and about the time of the event. It did not lead him to suggest that the event itself was unhistorical. In other words, Origen was no longer as sure as he once had been that he could differentiate myth and fiction from history.

[1] On Josephus see p. 115. In Origen's text of Josephus there was no description of the work of Jesus.

[2] Cleansing: Matthew, Mark, Luke against John; anointing Matthew, Mark, John against Luke.

It is therefore evident that, while Origen's mind did change as he considered the historical problems to be found in the gospels, it did not change simply because of theological presuppositions or a conservatism produced by age. It changed, at least in part, because he continued to apply the historical method taught by rhetoricians and used in his earlier works; he continued to apply it but he came to recognize its limitations. Indeed, as we have seen, he came to regard his earlier analysis of the incredibility of the cleansing story as "slavery to the letter", insistence upon the verbal details of the historical narrative at the expense of the reliability of the whole narrative.

We shall presently see that in his treatise *Contra Celsum* he pointed out that the method of κατασκευή, demonstration of the truth of a historical narrative, is exceedingly difficult to apply. We should add that he must have recognized that to demonstrate falsity was a task almost equally arduous. In his later works, then, he has come to realize that not all the problems of historical exegesis arise out of the texts. Some of them are provided by the method or methods involved.

A Different Approach—Contra Celsum

If new occasions teach new duties, we should expect to find Origen treating the gospel narratives differently when he came to write his reply to the *True Discourse* of the anti-Christian writer Celsus. In this reply he was no longer defending allegorical exegesis against simple believers and heretics who insisted on taking the gospel stories in a crudely literal way; he was defending the gospel stories themselves against an opponent whose way of looking at them was much like his own. And this opponent had said that the gospels contained a good many examples of fictions and myths.[1] What was Origen to do, when he himself, though using a different terminology, had expounded the same doctrine?

In the first place, he could insist upon the importance of exact scholarship and could criticize a few minor inaccuracies in Celsus'

[1] *C* 3, 27, p. 224.

account. "Those who practise avoiding mistakes take great pains to search and examine the statements on each subject and give their opinion rather slowly and carefully when they are deciding that one group of people is telling the truth and another telling falsehood in their narratives about miraculous happenings. For not all men give clear evidence of their credibility, nor do all men make it manifest that they have told men fictions and myths."[1] He could also insist upon the importance of philosophical presuppositions in dealing with such narratives. Naturalistic philosophers can criticize miracle stories; others should not do so.[2]

But while these arguments undoubtedly have their place in creating an atmosphere favourable to Origen's case, he recognizes that they do not answer the charges Celsus makes. The only answer, after all, to historical criticism is more historical criticism. A scorpion is no substitute for an egg. In the second place, therefore, he proceeds to discuss the nature of historical criticism itself, with a reference to the traditional rhetorical method of κατασκευή, "confirmation" of the truth of a story. "An attempt to substantiate (κατασκευάζειν) the truth of almost any story as historical fact, even if the story is true, and to produce complete certainty (καταληπτική φαντασία, a Stoic term) about it, is one of the most difficult tasks and in some cases is impossible."[3]

Here Origen is probably referring to the famous Eleventh Oration of the rhetorician Dio Chrysostom, who, as we have seen, argues on the basis of ἀνασκευή, "refutation", that neither *Iliad* nor *Odyssey* was true, and began with the words, "I know that to teach all men is difficult, while to deceive them is easy". But while Dio had rejected the historical character of the Homeric poems altogether, Origen followed another method of Homeric exegesis according to which the poems were partly true and partly false. Historical facts were to be found in them, but there were also "woven in" mythical and fictitious elements.[4] So he goes on to speak of the Trojan war, into which were "woven" impossible stories (i.e. myths) about sons of the gods and

[1] *C* 5, 57, p. 60; tr. H. Chadwick.
[2] Cf. *Miracle and Natural Law* (Amsterdam, 1952), pp. 199–200.
[3] *C* 1, 42, p. 92.
[4] Cf. Strabo, *Geog.* 1, 2, 9, c. 20; *The Letter and the Spirit*, pp. 95, 102.

fictitious stories (πλάσματα) about Oedipus and Jocasta, fictitious because of the mention of the Sphinx.¹ These references probably come from some Stoic manual on Homeric exegesis. But they cannot be discounted as simply taken over by Origen from a source he followed. The point he is making is completely dependent upon the analogy he has drawn between Greek mythology and its analysis and the gospels and their analysis.

This fact becomes clear as he draws his conclusion. "Anyone who reads the stories with a fair mind who wants to keep himself from being deceived by them will decide what he will accept and what he will interpret allegorically, searching out the meaning of the authors who wrote such fictitious stories, and what he will disbelieve as having been written to gratify certain people. We have said this by way of introduction to the whole question of the narrative about Jesus in the gospels."² The authors, then, are the evangelists. The "certain people" who are being "gratified" by the gospel narratives, literally interpreted, must be simple believers. And the fair-minded reader is the critic like Origen who is able to decide what is true and what is not.

What is true? Origen has already attacked Celsus' story that "the mother of Jesus was turned out by the carpenter who was betrothed to her, as she had been convicted of adultery and had a child by a certain soldier named Panthera".³ Origen regards this story as a "myth", but uses it as proof that his opponent recognizes the fact that Joseph was not the father of Jesus. He then proceeds to argue that the story of virginal conception is appropriate in regard to Jesus. According to Pythagoras, Plato, and Empedocles, "there are certain secret principles by which each soul that enters a body does so in accordance with its merits and former character". Furthermore, according to the physiognomists such as Zopyrus, Loxus, and Polemon, "all bodies conform to the habits of their souls".⁴ These remarks show that the virginal conception was "necessary".

---

¹ The Sphinx is fictitious according to Palaephatus (*De incred.* 4, pp. 10–12 Festa), whose work was used by rhetoricians like Theon (p. 96, 4–6 Spengel); cf. Dio Chrysostom (*Or.* 11, 8).

² *C* 1, 42, p. 93.　³ *C* 1, 32, p. 83.　⁴ 1, 33, p. 85.

But was the virginal conception possible? Celsus compared the story with Greek myths about Danae, Melanippe, Auge, and Antiope; Origen is willing to add the birth of Plato, son of Apollo and Amphictione, but says that all of them are mythological.[1] In order to prove the possibility he speaks of it as "credibility" of the virginal conception of Jesus, he mentions female animals which conceive spontaneously, such as the vulture, and the Greek notion that the first men came into existence from "generative principles" in the earth.[2]

It is after this discussion that he speaks of the dove at Jesus' baptism and explains the method of κατασκευή, which he is employing. Celsus thinks that the story about the dove (Luke 3.22) at Jesus' baptism is a fiction.[3] Here Origen really agrees with him. The descent of the dove and the opening of the heavens were certainly not perceptible to the senses.[4] But he has to insist that the story of the spiritual event is true, and he therefore suggests that Jesus probably told his disciples about his inner experience. Alternatively, one might say that "not all those who recorded the accounts of the form of the dove and the voice from heaven heard Jesus describing these things; but the Spirit that taught Moses the history before his time ... also taught the writers of the gospel about this miracle which occurred at the time of Jesus' baptism".[5] What this sentence means is that Luke's statement about the "corporeal form" of the Spirit probably does not come from Jesus himself but is a fictitious addition, inspired by the Spirit in order to point beyond corporeality.

Other points at which Celsus accuses the evangelists of writing fiction cause Origen less embarrassment. He is able to argue that hostile critics are more likely to write fiction than are the sincere disciples of Jesus,[6] and he can claim that when Celsus treats Judas' betrayal as fact but his repentance as fiction he is being inconsistent. Indeed, Celsus' own argument is "incredible".[7]

---

[1] 1, 37, p. 89.
[2] He probably speaks of credibility rather than of possibility because he does not wish to insist upon the factual nature of his parallels (he certainly does not himself accept the Greek story about the first men).
[3] C 1, 40, p. 90.   [4] J fr. 20. pp. 499–501.
[5] C 1, 44, p. 94.   [6] C 2, 10. p. 138.   [7] 2, 11, p. 139.

Again, Celsus claims that the disciples wrote fiction when they said that Jesus foreknew and foretold what was going to happen to him. Evidently he is referring to the passion-predictions often questioned by modern scholars. Origen replies that Jesus also predicted the persecution of his disciples; and such predictions are so unusual that they must be true. If these are true, Jesus' prediction of his own death is also true.[1] Moreover, if the evangelists were writing fiction they would hardly have recorded Jesus' predictions of the denial of Peter or the defection of the disciples.[2] Origen's basic point here is that since the disciples had no motive for reporting matters discreditable to themselves, their accounts of these matters must be true. As he says of the Gethsemane scene—which Celsus accepted but regarded as shameful[3]—"to conceal tales of this sort was easy, by not recording them at all".[4] In other words the Christian narratives are not "prejudicial".

Again, Celsus regarded the stories of Jesus' raising people from the dead as fictitious. Origen replies that "if it were fiction, many would have been described as rising, and those who had already spent more time in the tombs". Actually, however, there are only three such cases in the gospels: the daughter of the synagogue chief (Luke 8.49–56), the only son of the widow (Luke 7.11–17), and Lazarus, who had been in the tomb four days (John 11.1–44).[5] From Origen's other writings it is not altogether clear just how literally he took these stories. Of the first he says that while simple believers marvel at miracles, it is more important to consider that the girl symbolizes the synagogue of the Jews.[6] We do not possess his comments on the second. And Eustathius of Antioch bitterly criticizes Origen's exegesis of the story of Lazarus.[7] Origen, he says, should have glorified the great power of Christ and should have used it as proof of his deity; but he said nothing relevant to this purpose and instead treated Lazarus allegorically (ἀνήγαγεν) as a man who was sick and, indeed, dead in sins. Once more, we find that Origen's basic

---

[1] C 2, 13, pp. 141–2.   [2] C 2, 15, p. 144.   [3] 2, 24, p. 153.
[4] 2, 26, p. 155.   [5] C 2, 48, pp. 169–70.   [6] L fr. 15, pp. 239–40.
[7] Eustathius, De engastr. 21; Migne, PG 18, 656D; J fr. 63a, pp. 540–1.

concern is with what he considers the spirit, not the letter, of the miracle.

Moreover, in the very passage in which he lists the three raisings from the dead, he indicates that there is a hidden meaning in the words, "She is not dead but asleep" (Luke 8.52)[1], and he adds that the miracles took place in order to "lead many to the marvellousness of the doctrine of the gospel". In accordance with the promise of Jesus (John 14.12), however, the disciples later performed greater works than the sense-perceptible miracles which Jesus accomplished.[2]

Finally, we find that Celsus criticized the stories of the resurrection of Jesus himself. He began his attack by arguing that the resurrection resembled the tricks of ancient "divine men" who were trying "to convince simple hearers whom they exploit by deceit". He then suggested that no one "who really died ever rose again with the same body", and proceeded to criticize the Christian story. If other stories are myths, why should the Christian account be regarded as "noble and convincing"? What of Jesus' "cry from the cross when he expired, and the earthquake and the darkness"?

> While he was alive he did not help himself, but after death he rose again and showed the marks of his punishment and how his hands had been pierced. But who saw this? A hysterical female, as you say, and perhaps some other one of those who were deluded by the same sorcery, who either dreamt in a certain state of mind and through wishful thinking had a hallucination due to some mistaken notion (an experience which has happened to thousands), or, which is more likely wanted to impress the others by telling this fantastic tale, and so by this cock-and bull story to provide a chance for other beggars.[3]

Origen denies that the Greek stories are analogous, for Jesus was in fact crucified publicly; he really died—and rose. And for Jews and Christians alike resurrection is an unquestionable dogma. The earthquake and the darkness can be confirmed from the historical narrative of Phlegon of Tralles.[4]

---

[1] Christians do not die but sleep (*M* fr. 185–6, pp. 88–9).
[2] *C* 2, 48, p. 170. Cf. *Is. hom.* 6, 4, p. 274 Baehrens.
[3] *C* 2, 55, tr. Chadwick.
[4] *C* 2, 56–9, pp. 180–2. But elsewhere Origen denies that this is so; see p. 97.

As for the resurrection witnesses, they might have experienced hallucination had the event occurred at night. "But his idea of a vision in the daytime is not convincing when the people were in no way mentally unbalanced and were not suffering from delirium or melancholy." There is no evidence in the gospels to show that Mary Magdalene was hysterical.[1]

Unfortunately for Celsus' own consistency, he goes on to criticize the nature of the resurrection appearances by saying that "after his death, Jesus used to produce only a mental impression of the wounds he received on the cross, and did not really appear wounded in this way". Origen has no difficulty in pointing out that according to John 20.25-7, Jesus appeared and showed his wounds to Thomas, a disciple "who did not believe and thought the miracle to be impossible".[2]

Another objection was that "if Jesus really wanted to show forth divine power, he ought to have appeared to the very men who treated him despitefully and to the man who condemned him and to everyone everywhere". Origen replies by making use of his theory that Jesus did not always appear in the same way to everyone; he had several aspects, which differed in proportion to the spiritual levels of the witnesses.[3] Celsus also argued that "if he really was so great he ought, in order to display his divinity, to have disappeared suddenly from the cross". Origen's main answer to this objection is based on the question of fact. To be sure, Jesus could have disappeared in this way, but he did not do so. And if he had done so, Celsus would doubtless have asked, "Why did he disappear after arriving at the cross, when he did not do this before his passion?" And in Origen's view Celsus actually ends with absurdity. He says that "when he was punished he was seen by all, but by only one person after he rose again, whereas the opposite ought to have happened". The "opposite" would be for him to have been seen by one person at the crucifixion and by all after the resurrection. But this would be "impossible and irrational".[4]

---

[1] 2, 60, p. 183. Presumably Celsus recalls that according to Luke 8.2 seven demons had emerged from her.

[2] 2, 61, p. 183.   [3] See Chapter 4, pp. 80-1; C 2, 63-7, pp. 184-9.

[4] 2, 68-70, pp. 189-93.

At another point in his treatise Celsus discussed the angelic visitations recorded in the gospels and therefore touched upon the resurrection story once more.[1]

> They say that an angel came to the tomb of this very man (some say one angel, some two), who replied to the women that he was risen. The Son of God, it seems, was not able to open the tomb, but needed someone else to move the stone.

Origen replies that the gospels do not disagree as much as Celsus supposes. Matthew (28.2) and Mark (16.5) do have one angel, while Luke (24.4) and John (20.12) have two. But "the writers that have one angel say that this one was he who rolled back the stone from the sepulchre, whereas those that have two say they stood in shining raiment before the women who came to the tomb, or that they were seen 'sitting in white robes' within it".[2] The story is historically true. When Celsus speaks of the inability of the Son of God to roll away the stone, he is "like a young fellow at school who has been given the task of pulling some argument to pieces". In other words, he is using the method of ἀνασκευή at a point where Origen regards it as inappropriate. Origen replies that it is "more dignified" for an inferior servant to have moved the stone than for the rising Lord to have done so. Furthermore, the story contains a philosophical allegory.[3]

Obviously Origen is using the method of κατασκευή in all these instances, and he is trying to substantiate the historical truth of the narratives. In the last examples we have cited, he is evidently trying to prove that the physical body of Jesus was raised from the dead—or so it appears.

But as usual he is presenting only one aspect of his doctrine. Especially in his earlier works he was always anxious to avoid the errors both of heretics, who denied a bodily resurrection altogether (and he could see that Celsus' approach was similar to theirs) and of the simpler believers, who believed in the resurrection of the physical body.[4] In the early treatise *On the Resurrection* Origen carefully explained that human bodies are composed of the four elements: earth, water, air, and fire.[5] Then he went on to

---

[1] 5, 52, p. 56. [2] 5, 56, p. 59. [3] 5, 58, p. 61.
[4] Lommatzsch 17, 61–2. [5] Ibid., 62.

say that the body of Jesus was different from that of human beings, since it was not born of the seed of a man and the pleasure of the flesh. He did eat and drink after the resurrection, but he did not conceal the nature of the body which was made of air and was spiritual.[1] The form of his body remained the same, but the substance was different.[2] And such a doctrine was not abandoned by Origen in his old age. In *Contra Celsum* he says that Jesus' resurrection body was on the borderline between the density (παχύτης) it possessed before the passion and the way it would appear as a naked soul.[3] It is worth noting that Origen never refers to the words of Luke 24.39 about the flesh and bones of the risen Jesus, even though he does say that Jesus "evidently seems to have eaten some fish after his resurrection".[4]

How "positive" is Origen's historical treatment of the life of Jesus when he writes against Celsus? Certainly he defends the stories of the virginal conception, the descent of the dove, the resurrections of dead persons. Jesus predicted his own passion and the defection of his disciples; Judas really betrayed him, though later, like the other disciples, he repented. But when Origen speaks of miracles he betrays a certain hesitation—not so much in the case of virginal conception, for which he knows pagan parallels (thus he reverses the attitude of modern writers) as in the cases of the dove's descent and of resurrections. His position in regard to the resurrection of Jesus, the cardinal and undeniable miracle, is not ambiguous, though it seemed so to literalists in antiquity. There is reason to suppose that he did not regard the resurrection of Jesus as "physical"—but at the same time he undoubtedly regarded it as historical.

ORIGEN AND THE HISTORICAL METHOD
Summary

We have seen that Origen regarded the refutation of a narrative ostensibly historical as a task much easier than its confirmation. This view was based partly on the nature of the method he used,

---

[1] Ibid., 65.　　[2] Epiphanius, *Haer.* 64, 14, 9—15, 1, p. 424, Holl.
[3] 2, 62, p. 184.　　[4] *C* 1, 70, p. 124; John 21.13.

78

taken over from the schools of rhetoric, and partly on his theological purpose, which involved the refutation of a good deal of "the letter" so that the "spirit" could be revealed. Origen was not interested in what he called "mere" history. He was a philosophical theologian who used history only where history suited his theological purposes. Indeed, there is considerable justification for claiming that he was primarily concerned not with history but with the historical method; it was his misfortune that the historical method he used was ultimately inadequate.

His use of the historical method of his time is most clearly evident in those books of his *Commentary on John* which he wrote just after leaving Alexandria for Caesarea. Presumably he felt that he had been released from the pressures placed upon him by the bishop and the simple literalists in Egypt; now he could employ his method as thoroughly as possible and could search the scriptures for their allegorical meaning. Over a period of time, however, he came to regard his method somewhat less highly. He had once come close to denying the historical nature of at least the first four chapters of John; later he corrected his own interpretation, at least in regard to the cleansing of the temple, and came to recognize, at least in part, the limitations of the method he had been using.

4

ORIGEN AND THE LIFE OF JESUS

THE MINISTRY AND PERSON OF JESUS

GIVEN the existence of the synoptic and the Johannine portraits of Jesus, and the partial explanation of their differences as due to their emphases on the humanity and on the divinity of Jesus, it was still necessary for Origen to explain how it was that the portraits could be as different as they were. In the second century there had been many Christians, especially gnostics, who were unable to believe that a divine being could have become incarnate; they argued that the Christ had merely seemed to be born, to suffer, and to die. In their view the miracles proved Christ's divinity; nothing proved his humanity. And in writings fairly close to such speculation we find the idea that Jesus appeared in different forms at different times to different persons.[1] From "tradition" Clement informs us that sometimes, when the beloved disciple reclined in Jesus' bosom, there was nothing tangible on which he could rest.[2]

Origen was undoubtedly influenced by such traditional information, but the real point of departure for his thought lay in the gospels themselves, where he could find a link with John in the synoptic story of the transfiguration. This story shows that "the Logos has different forms".[3] And because Matthew (17.2) and Mark (9.2) say that Jesus was transfigured "in the presence of" the three disciples, while Luke (9.29) states only that "the form of his person became different", it is possible that he was transfigured before some but, at the same time, not before others.[4] The reason for this must be that the evangelists are describing a spiritual vision, not one perceptible to the senses.[5] Each witness saw Jesus in proportion to his spiritual comprehension.[6]

In Origen's view the transfiguration story was the key to the

[1] *Acta Iohannis* 93, pp. 195–6 Bonnet; W. Bauer, *Das Leben Jesu*, pp. 313–14.
[2] *Hypotyp.* frag. 24, p. 210 Stählin.   [3] *M* 12, 36, p. 152.   [4] *M* 12, 37, p. 153.
[5] *C* 4, 16, pp. 285–6.   [6] *C* 6, 77, pp. 146–9.

ways in which the disciples saw Jesus, not only at that time but always. As the Logos, Jesus was like the Old Testament manna which turned into whatever each person desired (here Origen follows Philo).[1] And such metamorphoses took place both corporeally and in relation to the nature of the Logos, which does not appear in the same way to all.[2] The notion that Jesus' physical appearance changed is, of course, based on the story of the transfiguration, as well as on Luke's story of the resurrection appearance on the road to Emmaus. The disciples did not recognize him at first (Luke 24.16)—for he was seen by them "as they were able to see".[3] Moreover, the theory explains why it was necessary for Judas to identify Jesus for the soldiers who arrested him; they could not tell who he was "because of his metamorphoses".[4]

Evidently this theory, in spite of its possible meaningfulness in relation to spiritual edification,[5] and its implicit insistence on the subjectivity of the evangelists (sometimes explicit),[6] leaves historical understanding in ruins. The Jesus of whom Origen speaks is finally neither God nor man but, in his phrase, "a sort of composite being".[7]

But Origen does not always adhere to this theory. Indeed, most of the time he treats the various gospels as records of historical events. And we must therefore turn to his analyses of the gospel stories in order to see what he makes of their account of the life of Jesus.

The different genealogies of Jesus in Matthew and Luke presented a problem. Julius Africanus had militantly rejected the notion that both were fictitious and were composed in praise of Jesus. False praise of God is false, and therefore the genealogies have to be reconciled. By using several ingenious hypotheses Africanus was able to reconcile them.[8] Origen, on the other hand, was content to point out that the persons mentioned in the

---

[1] Cf. the note of Klostermann on *M* 100, p. 218.   [2] *M* 100, pp. 218–19.
[3] *L* fr. 85, p. 274.   [4] *M* 100.
[5] F. Bertrand, *Mystique de Jésus chez Origène* (Paris, 1951), pp. 14–46.
[6] *J* 1, 6, p. 8.   [7] *C* 1, 66, p. 119.
[8] Cf. W. Reichardt, *Die Briefe des Sextus Julius Africanus an Aristides und Origenes* (*TU* 34, 3, Leipzig, 1909).

genealogies are different; that the genealogies are arranged in descending order in Matthew, in ascending order in Luke; and that Luke, who places the genealogy after Jesus' baptism, does not include any women in it.[1] He then turns to the allegorical meaning which must be sought because the gospels disagree.

A spiritual meaning could be found in Matthew's genealogy[2] as well as in Luke's, for Origen insists that the word γένησις in Matt. 1.1 is different from the word γέννησις in Matt. 1.18. The former refers to "the first formation from God"; the latter, to the "consecutive descent from condemnation to death because of the transgression".[3] This distinction is not very solidly based, since the best manuscripts read γένησις at both points; but the reading of Irenaeus was the same as that which Origen followed.

Origen insisted upon the historical actuality of the virginal conception, though at times he recognized it as a "mystery" of faith.[4] He was willing to accept the testimony of apocryphal gospels in order to defend the perpetual virginity of Mary; the so-called brothers of Jesus, he says, were sons of Joseph by a previous marriage.[5] They were called brothers by a legal fiction.[6] By providing two Old Testament examples (Isa. 46.4; Gen. 8.7) in which "until" could be translated as "constantly", Origen was able to explain Matt. 1.25 as meaning that Joseph "did not know" Mary—i.e., know the source of her conceiving—"at any time when she had given birth, and he saw the signs which took place".[7] This exegesis is rather strained.[8]

Origen gives no precise day for Jesus' birth, possibly because in his view only the unrighteous are described in scripture as observing their birthdays.[9] There is a fragment ascribed both to Origen and Eusebius[10] in which an attempt is made to reconcile the divergent chronological data about Jesus' infancy found in

---

[1] L 28, pp. 172–3.
[2] Matthew's genealogy must be taken spiritually since literally it disagrees with data given in 2 Kings (*Rom. comm.*, PG 14, 850C–1C).
[3] M fr. 11, pp. 19–20.   [4] M fr. 281, p. 126.
[5] M 10, 17, pp. 21–2 (*Nativity of Mary* 9, 2, p. 19 Testuz).
[6] J fr. 31, p. 506.   [7] M fr. 22, p. 24.   [8] Cf. L 7, p. 49.
[9] M 10, 22, p. 30; from Philo, cf. Hanson, *Allegory and Event*, p. 249 n8.
[10] M fr. 23, p. 25.

Matthew and in Luke; but we may probably suppose that the information given in it does not come from Origen.[1]

As for the important question of the duration of Jesus' ministry, Origen changed his mind on this subject. In his earlier writings, when he inclined to regard historical information found in John as almost purely allegorical, he accepted the synoptic chronology and held that Jesus preached the gospel for a year and a few months[2] or, less precisely, for a year.[3] When he came to regard the historical value of John more highly he stated that the ministry lasted about three years[4] and Judas' discipleship not quite three years.[5] His reconciliation of John with the synoptics cannot be regarded very highly, since in his later period he implied that Jesus was crucified in the fifteenth year of Tiberius[6] and stated that he was in the world for thirty years.[7] Here he was giving information derived from the gospel of Luke (3.1,23) but neither examining it critically nor correlating it with the gospel of John.[8]

Origen was not really interested in chronology, as we shall see when we come to his remarks on the date of the crucifixion. He explains the star which led the Magi as "like a comet"; he refers to the treatise on comets by the Stoic Chaeremon to show that comets are sometimes portents of good events to come;[9] but he does not make any effort to state when the "comet" might have appeared.

When he deals with the story of the boy Jesus in the temple (Luke 2.41–52) he provides a kind of psychological analysis of it. Luke 2.48 has Mary say to Jesus, "Behold, your father and I have been looking for you anxiously." This saying cannot be taken literally. Mary knew about the virginal conception; Joseph too must have known in view of Matthew's story of the nativity. They knew that Jesus was divine. Therefore they must have been afraid that Jesus had returned to heaven. Moreover, the story

---

[1] The Magi visited Jesus when he was two years old; then he was taken to Egypt, and remained there until he was four, in the forty-fifth year of Augustus and the first year of Archelaus. The two years named are not identical.

[2] *P* 4, 1, 5, p. 299.   [3] *L* 32, p. 195.   [4] *M* 40, p. 79.

[5] *C* 2, 12, p. 141.   [6] *M* 40.   [7] *M* 78, p. 188.

[8] Cf. Bauer, op. cit., 287–8.   [9] *C* 1, 58–9, pp. 109–10.

shows that "the Father's house" (Luke 2.49) is the temple; therefore the Father of Jesus was God, not Joseph.[1] Elsewhere Origen has already explained that Joseph was called the father of Jesus because he was his guardian.[2]

We have already discussed Jesus' baptism and temptation when in dealing with the Johannine-synoptic contradictions. Here it should be added that Origen did not think that the three temptations described by Matthew and Luke took place during the forty days of fasting. What of the forty days' temptations in Mark? They were not described by the evangelists, probably because they were "greater than could be written".[3]

A severe chronological difficulty arises when one considers the sequence of events after the temptations. In John Jesus is not tempted but calls his disciples near Bethany, then goes via Cana to Capernaum, and finally cleanses the temple in Jerusalem (John 1.35—2.22). The Baptist has not yet been imprisoned (3.24). In Matthew and Luke Jesus goes first to Nazareth, then to Capernaum; in Matthew and Mark he begins his journey after John's imprisonment; by the sea of Galilee (Matthew, Mark) or the lake of Gennesaret (Luke) he calls his disciples.

First we should notice that Origen tries to clear up some of the minor topographical difficulties. The text of John 1.28, he says, should not read "Bethany" but "Bethabara". He himself has made a pilgrimage to the holy land, and he knows that Bethany is only fifteen stadia from Jerusalem, while the Jordan river is 180 stadia farther.[4] Again, one might suppose that the sea of Galilee is different from the lake of Gennesaret; actually they are the same, and one can also use the name "sea of Tiberias", as in John 6.1.[5]

But, literally understood, the texts still present difficulties. Origen rather tentatively suggests that the different accounts of the call of Simon Peter in John and the synoptics refer to different

---

[1] *L* 19, pp. 127–8. [2] *nutricius, L* 16, p. 107; *L* 17, p. 111.

[3] *L* 29, p. 178; cf. John 21. 25. The same explanation is given in regard to the Lucan summary of the Baptist's proclamation (Luke 3.18; *L* 27, pp. 168–70) and the fact that not all parables are interpreted by the evangelists (*M* 14, 12, p. 304).

[4] *J* 6, 40, p. 149. He uses the distance from Bethany to Jerusalem (found in John 11.18) to prove that the triumphal entry must be allegorized (*J* 10, 27, p. 200).

[5] *M* 11, 18, p. 65; *L* fr. 3, p. 233.

persons,[1] but there are further "discords in relation to the letter". The synoptic—Johannine contradictions lead the reader to suppose that none of the stories can be taken literally.[2] And there are further difficulties within one of the synoptics. Luke has Jesus go first to Nazareth, then to Capernaum; but in Nazareth we find a reference to works already done in Capernaum. Therefore, the story contains a "mystery"; and the simplest solution, in Origen's view, is to regard Nazareth as equivalent to the Jews, Capernaum to the gentiles.[3]

Origen does not care for the old gnostic exegesis of Jesus' descent to Capernaum (Luke 4.31; John 2.12) as representing his coming down to the material world.[4] He insists that according to the synoptic gospels Jesus performed many real actions in the city.[5] But he also recommends the compilation from the four gospels of everything written about Capernaum—"the words and works of the Lord there, how often he stayed there, when he is said to have descended to it, when gone into it, and whence".[6] The allegorical meaning is about to make its appearance. Indeed, Daniélou has pointed out that Origen seems to take over Gnostic allegorization when he suggests that the "brothers" of Jesus in John 2.12 are actually "powers" which had come down with him.[7] Because of Origen's insistence upon the perpetual virginity of Mary, the "brothers" were obviously not really brothers.

We have seen that at the time he wrote his Commentary on John Origen accepted practically nothing in the second chapter as historical. Some geographical details remained valid: thus Capernaum and Jerusalem were certainly places, and Cana (though most of Origen's comments on John 2.1–11 are lost) was probably a place too. We do not know what Origen made of the historical setting provided in the third chapter of John, for the portions of his commentary which dealt with it have not survived; it is at least possible, however, that he treated it symbolically.

Origen's treatment of the fourth chapter of John reflects his

[1] *J* 10, 8, pp. 177–8.   [2] *J* 10, 3–5, pp. 172–6.   [3] *L* 33, p. 196.

[4] *J* 10, 11, p. 180. Marcion in A. v. Harnack, *Marcion: das Evangelium vom fremden Gott* (2nd ed., Leipzig, 1924), pp. 184*–5*; cf. *The Letter and the Spirit*, p. 64 n7.

[5] *J* 10, 11–12, pp. 180–2.   [6] *J* 10, 12, p. 182.

[7] *J* 10, 9, pp. 178–9; J. Daniélou, *Origène* (Paris, 1948), pp. 191–2.

determination to show that it is essentially unhistorical. He reads in John 4.1 that the Pharisees know about Jesus' work of baptizing; but in the synoptic gospels Jesus nowhere baptizes—and, in addition, John 4.2 states that Jesus himself did not baptize. Moreover, John disagrees with the synoptics as to the time of the Baptist's imprisonment.[1] Therefore, since the accounts differ in regard both to actions and to times, the Johannine account must be regarded as symbolical. Again, in John 4.35 Jesus asks, "Do you not say, There are yet four months, then comes the harvest?" Origen treats this quotation as a literal indication of time.[2] In Judaea the harvest begins either in Nisan or Iyar; in either case, when we subtract four months we get back to winter. Was John 4.35 spoken in the winter? No, it was not. The Passover mentioned in John 2.13–15 (and Passover was observed in Nisan) is mentioned in John 4.45 as having taken place quite recently; the Galilaeans have clear memories of it. Origen is insisting upon, and, indeed, exaggerating the importance of the sequence of historical events, so that he can take the text allegorically.[3] He is claiming that since the story is chronologically incoherent it cannot be taken literally. And, though he does not say so at this point, he apparently believed (as he was writing on John) that the ministry of Jesus lasted only about one year. Johannine chronology was therefore *a priori* unacceptable.

In dealing with Jesus' reception in Galilee Origen was impressed by the lack of logical continuity in John 4.43–5. There he read that Jesus went to Galilee, *for* he himself testified that a prophet has no honour in his own country; when he came to Galilee, the Galilaeans welcomed him. Since the sequence of ideas does not make sense, Origen concluded that both Judaea and Galilee must be symbols rather than names of real places.[4]

He also pointed out that there are historical difficulties in the story of the son of the royal officer (βασιλικός) in John 4.46–54. Here Origen's comments seem rather inconclusive, probably because it was difficult to provide much real evidence against the historicity of the account. He tries to show that it is difficult

[1] *J* 10, 8, p. 178.   [2] See also *Rom. Comm.* 3, 7 (*PG* 14, 943B).
[3] *J* 13, 39, pp. 264–5.   [4] *J* 13, 54, pp. 283–4.

to identify a βασιλικός. The more simple-minded reader, he says, may suppose that the βασιλικός served Herod, or perhaps that he was someone of Caesar's household. It is not clear whether he was a Jew or not. He did have high rank because his slaves are mentioned in the plural. Since in this context Origen also discusses the similar story (Matt. 8.5–13) of the centurion's son or servant, we assume that his basic purpose was to show how difficult it was to identify the centurion with the βασιλικός or, for that matter, to draw any historical conclusion at all. Actually both the βασιλικός and his son are symbols, and Origen agrees with Heracleon that the father is one of the "archons" of the "aeon".[1] Here Origen has provided exceedingly flimsy grounds for joining the Valentinians in their allegorization of the stories.[2]

But there is a difference between the gnostics and Origen. In the first place, the content of their exegesis is not simply identical with his. In the second place, he finds it necessary, as apparently they did not, to prove that the passages he deals with must be taken allegorically. The method he uses, as we have already seen, is that of ἀνασκευή. In the story of the Samaritan woman, the time is wrong; in that of Jesus' journey to Galilee, the reason assigned is incredible; and in that of the royal officer, the identity of the person involved is obscure. He has shown, at least to a reader acquainted with his method, that the narratives contained in the fourth chapter of John are at least improbable (fictions) or, at most, false (myths). To use his own terminology, we should say they are either parables or enigmas (cf. p. 66).

In Origen's view, then, the first four chapters of the gospel of John cannot be reconciled with the synoptics, and they contain internal inconsistencies which prove that they must be taken not literally but allegorically. The fact that the "Bethabara" of John 1.28 is a real place does not prove that the events located were perceptible to the senses, any more than the fact that there was a real temple in Jerusalem proves that it was cleansed. At least in the stage in his thinking represented by this part of the Commentary on John, Origen regarded the contents of its opening

---

[1] J13, 57, p. 288; 13, 62, p. 295; Daniélou, op cit., p. 192.
[2] Cf. Irenaeus, Adv. haer. 1, 7, 5, p. 64.

chapters as unhistorical. We may recall that Tatian felt free to rearrange the sequence of narratives in the first five chapters of John. (We do not know what Origen did with the fifth chapter since his commentary on it is lost.)

On the other hand, when all four gospels do agree he accepts their historical character. The feeding of the five thousand is recorded not only in the sixth chapter of John but also in the synoptic gospels. Origen points out that in some details the stories are not in agreement; thus the boy with five barley loaves and two fish (John 6.9) is not mentioned by the synoptists. But he has no doubts about the reality of the miracle, at least by the time he writes his *Commentary on Matthew*. (Once more, his comment on the Johannine version has not survived.) Why did Jesus "look up" to the heavens? "With the rays of his eyes he was, so to speak drawing down power from there which would be mixed with the loaves and the fish." Moreover, he "blesses" the food. By this word of blessing he was "increasing and multiplying" it, as in the account of God's blessing at creation in Gen. 1.28.[1]

Of course there are symbolical details in the Johannine discourse which follows the miracle. The verse about eating the flesh of the Son of Man and drinking his blood (John 6.53) is a New Testament example of the letter which kills (2 Cor. 3.6).[2] Origen insists upon a more spiritual interpretation of the Eucharist.[3]

There was not just one feeding, as in John and Luke, for in Origen's opinion the feeding of the four thousand (Matt. 15.32–9) is a separate and distinct narrative about another event. In the story of the five thousand, the disciples tell Jesus that it is evening, and he asks them about the food they have; it consists of five loaves and two fish. The crowds recline on the grass, and Jesus blesses the food. In the story of the four thousand, Jesus speaks to the disciples about the crowd that has been with him for three days; there are seven loaves and a few fish. The crowd falls down on the ground, and Jesus gives thanks.[4] Indeed, Origen

---

[1] *M* 11, 2, p. 36.   [2] *Lev. hom.* 7, 5, p. 387 *Baehrens.*   [3] *J* 32, 24, p. 468.
[4] *M* 11, 19, pp. 67–8.

hints that there may be three stories of feeding, for John describes the miracle as taking place in the mountains.[1] His final conclusion, however, is that there were two.[2]

Another miracle which Origen discusses in considerable detail is the healing of an epileptic child (Matt. 17.14–21; Mark 9.14–29; Luke 9.37–43). In dealing with the story he points out that it belongs to a class of healings in which people ask for others to be aided; other examples are the centurion's servant (Matt. 8.5–13; Luke 7.1–10); the royal officer's son (John 4.46–54); Jairus' daughter (Matt. 9.18–26; Mark 5.21–43; Luke 8.40–56); and the Canaanite's daughter (Matt. 15.21–8; Mark 7.24–30). In another kind of story Jesus acts on his own initiative, as in the case of the man who had been paralysed for thirty-eight years (John 5.2–9). These stories show that the miracles are the result of divine power, not of faith alone.[3] The miracle itself, in this instance, was the expulsion of an evil spirit. To be sure, Matthew relates that the child's father said he was "a lunatic" (σεληνιάζεται), and medical men explain lunacy as due to waters in the head which move with the phases of the moon. It is possible that the unclean spirit observed these phases. But we "who believe the gospel" must hold that the case was not simple lunacy, since that can sometimes be cured by Egyptian incantations.[4]

Here Origen is combining insistence on the uniqueness of Jesus' healing ministry with "scientific" acceptance of both medicine and magic. The result is not especially fortunate. And since to this story Matthew has appended Jesus' saying about faith moving a mountain, indeed "this mountain" (17.20), Origen is mistakenly moved to interpret the mountain as the spirit which was in the lunatic.[5] Elsewhere he compares the working of faith in the moving of mountains to the "natural attraction" of a magnet to iron and of naphtha to fire.[6] At points like this we have to recognize that Origen was capable of nodding.

A different kind of problem was to be found at the point where Matthew (8.28) tells of two demoniacs who came out of tombs to meet Jesus, while Mark (5.2) and Luke (8.27) tell the

---

[1] P. 68; John 6.3. [2] C 2, 46, p. 168. [3] M 13, 3, p. 187; cf. 10, 19, p. 26.
[4] M 13, 6, pp. 193–4. [5] M 13, 7 .p. 197. [6] M 10, 19, p. 25.

story in greater detail but mention only one. Origen does not seem to recognize that it is characteristic of Matthew to describe pairs (9.27; 20.29). And at this point he does not make use of an allegorical explanation as he does in another instance where Matthew has two persons instead of the one found in Mark and Luke (see p. 93). Instead, he gives a purely literary interpretation. Matthew was writing "generically" about exorcisms and left out part of the story. Mark and Luke, concerned with an individual example, gave fuller details.[1]

The number of the demoniacs is not the only question which arises in relation to this story, which deals with demons which entered the bodies of swine and drove them from a cliff into the sea. Where was the cliff? At one point in his *Commentary on John* Origen tried to solve the geographical problem. The evangelists, who had accurate knowledge of Judaean geography, cannot have made a statement which was obviously false. Therefore when most of the manuscripts known to Origen located the miracle in "the country of the Gerasenes", their reading was corrupt; Gerasa is "a city of Arabia, in the vicinity of neither a sea nor a lake". Some manuscripts mentioned the "Gadarenes", but near Gadara there is neither a lake nor a cliff. Origen therefore felt free to substitute "Gergesenes", since Gergesa is a town by the lake of Tiberias (sea of Galilee). "Near it there is a cliff bordering on the lake, and from it one is shown that the swine were cast down by the demons." Since the name Gergesa means "habitation of those cast out", Origen feels that it must be substituted for either Gerasa or Gadara.[2]

By combining geographical information with symbolism Origen justifies a purely conjectural emendation of the gospel text.

PETER AND HIS CONFESSION

One of the crucial points in the synoptic gospels is the scene placed by Matthew and Mark near Caesarea Philippi, where the apostle Peter acknowledges Jesus as the Christ. Almost nothing is made of this scene by John, who alludes to the tradition only in

[1] *M* fr. 164, p. 81.   [2] *J* 6, 41, p. 150.

a couple of verses (6.68–9). We are therefore not surprised to find that Origen undertakes to minimize the importance of Peter in his treatment of the passage. According to Matt. 16.18–19 Jesus said to Peter, "on the rock (πέτρα) I will build my church". What is the rock? Origen carefully explains that the rock is "every imitator of Christ", and he goes on to argue that the rock cannot be identified as Peter. "If you think that on that one Peter alone the church is built, what of John the son of thunder, or each of the apostles? Did the gates of Hades prevail against the others?" Moreover, it is clear from John 20.22 that the Holy Spirit was given to all the disciples, not to Peter alone. Origen has to admit that according to the literal meaning of Matthew, the rock was Peter; but according to the spirit, it means everyone who becomes what Peter was.[1] He points out that both Mark and Luke "do not add" the words "Son of the living God" to "you are the Christ"; they do not add the blessing and the promise given by Jesus to Peter.[2] He may wish to say that something has been interpolated in Matthew's account. But his theory of the composition of the gospels prevents him from doing so, and in the absence of any textual variants of importance he cannot provide a more definite statement.

He is aware, however, of Peter's rebuke of Jesus, and he explains it as due to the apostle's imperfect knowledge. Peter had just begun to learn about Jesus' future suffering, which he regarded as unworthy of the Son of the living God; the prediction of suffering had not been revealed to him.[3] Actually this doctrine was absolutely essential, for it is necessary to preach "Jesus Christ crucified" (1 Cor. 2.2), and it is useless to preach him and to be silent about the cross. Indeed, it is more important to proclaim the crucifixion than to speak of the nativity, the star of Bethlehem, the angels, or the other miracles.[4] This remark seems to be directed against those who upheld the primacy of Peter and relied on the gospel of Matthew to prove it, for nativity, star, and angels are to be found in Matthew but not in John.

On the other hand, when Origen is not concerned with the

---

[1] M 12, 10–11, pp. 86–8.   [2] 12, 15, p. 105.
[3] M 12, 21, p. 116.   [4] 12, 19, pp. 111–12. Contrast J 32, 16, p. 452.

question of primacy he can treat Peter in quite a different way. In Matt. 18.18 Jesus speaks to the disciples about binding and loosing on earth and in heaven (ἐν οὐρανῷ). Is this the same as his similar statement to Peter in Matt. 16.19? No, it is not, says Origen. Peter received the keys of the kingdom "of the heavens" and what he bound or loosed on earth was to be bound or loosed "in the heavens" (ἐν τοῖς οὐρανοῖς). Therefore to him was given authority in more than one heaven—indeed, in all heavens.[1] Here Origen is minimizing the authority of the Church and maximizing that of Peter. He either forgets or, more probably, disregards what he has said earlier. Yet we must recall that in his view Peter was by no means as perfect as the disciple who reclined in the bosom of Jesus.

From Galilee to Jerusalem

Because of his detailed studies of the synoptic parallels, Origen was well aware that the sequence of events in Matt. 18.10ff. differs from that in Luke 9.51ff. To-day we explain this divergence as due to Luke's insertion of a collection of "travel-teachings" or "peripatetic teachings" between Mark 9.50 and Mark 10.1. Origen, as we have seen, did not believe that Luke used Mark and therefore could not explain the divergence. He was aware that Matt. 19.1–12 parallels Mark 10.1–12 (question of divorce) and that the blessing of the children (Matt. 19.13–15; Mark 10.13–16) has a Lucan parallel (Luke 18.15–17). And he knows that when the journey to Jerusalem really begins, Matthew and Mark agree as to the sequence of events, and Luke concurs in part. "As in most other cases, Matthew and Mark have the same order."[2] But even where the order is approximately the same, one must remember that there is a hidden meaning. Even if the story about Jesus' passage through Jericho is historically true, we should remember what Jericho and Jerusalem mean in the parable of the Good Samaritan; here, therefore, Jesus is depicted as passing from this world to the celestial Jerusalem.[3] Moreover, there are differences. Is Matt. 20.29–34 the equivalent of Mark 10.46–52

[1] *M* 13, 31, p. 270. [2] *M* 16, 8, pp. 490–1. [3] *M* 16, 9, pp. 501–3.

and Luke 18.35–43? If one considers "mere history" he will say there were three visits to Jericho because the details are so different. But there is a hidden meaning. The two blind men in Matthew are Israel and Judah; Mark alone mentions Bartimaeus and explains his name as "son of Timaeus" because of the merit (τίμιον) of the patriarch Jacob-Israel.[1] Moreover, Luke has Jesus draw near to Jericho; Mark has him go into it and come out of it; Matthew mentions only the going out. This has a mystical significance, since Jericho means the world. So in Luke the blind man asks who Jesus is; in Mark he hears that it is Jesus the Nazarene; in Matthew two hear that Jesus is passing by.

Since this story has a mystical significance, it was all the easier for Origen to insist that the story of the triumphal entry was allegorical too. As we have seen in his earlier work he was convinced that it was entirely allegorical. Later he came to believe that it was both literal and allegorical. He still insisted that conflicting details had to be taken symbolically.[2]

THE PASSION NARRATIVE

We have also seen that Origen insisted that the story of the anointing of Jesus was more mystical than historical—once more because of the disagreements of the evangelists. When he came to consider the last supper, however, he firmly held that it was a historical event to which a date could be given. To be sure, in the *Commentary on John* Origen said that Jesus died "on the Passover".[3] But in the *Commentary on Matthew* he seems to have changed his mind.[4] He feels free to say that while Jesus did actually eat the Passover on the fourteenth of Nisan, there is no reason for Christians to do so; they celebrate a new and spiritual Passover— Christ.[5] The disciples were eating "in accordance with the commandment of the law".[6]

The Gethsemane story is omitted by John, who is concerned more with Jesus' divinity than with his humanity and knows that

[1] *M* 16, 12, pp. 511–12.   [2] *M* 16, 14, pp. 520, 522.   [3] *J* 28, 25, p. 423.

[4] Bauer, op. cit., p. 162 n1, argues that in *J* 28, 25 *pascha* refers to the whole feast including the *azyma*; to me it seems more likely that Origen's mind changed.

[5] *M* 75, pp. 175–6; 76, p. 178; 79, pp. 188–9.   [6] *M* 80, p. 191. Cf. *C* 1, 70, p. 124.

God the Logos cannot be tempted and that God, who is impassible, cannot want to escape suffering.[1] Historically the scene was real, however. Only three disciples witnessed it because they were firmer in their faith than the others; and it was this scene that they witnessed so that they would not become over-confident about their own fidelity.[2]

Celsus, a generation earlier, had ridiculed the story of Gethsemane.[3]

> If these things had been decreed for him and if he was punished in obedience to his Father, it is obvious that since he was a god and acted intentionally, what was done of deliberate purpose was neither painful nor grievous to him. Why then does he utter loud laments and wailings, and pray that he may avoid the fear of death, saying something like this, "O Father, if this cup could pass by me"?

Origen replies that Jesus "assumed with the body also its pains and griefs". The story, therefore, is not inconsistent, logically or theologically. But what of Celsus' carping criticism of Jesus' actions and words? First, the gospels do not say that Jesus "uttered wailings".[4] Second, Celsus does not quote Jesus' words accurately; Jesus said, "Father, if it be possible, let this cup pass from me" (Matt. 26.39). Third, he quotes only the words which reflect the weakness of Jesus' human flesh, not those which refer to the willingness of his human spirit: "nevertheless, not as I will, but as thou wilt"—a sentiment expressed not once but twice (Matt. 26.39,42).

It could also be said that when Jesus was praying for the cup to pass from him he was not praying for himself but for the Jewish people, whom he wanted to save from their fate.[5] But Origen's main line of approach, at this point, is based upon the doctrine that Jesus really suffered human agonies; he did not merely seem to do so.

Origen draws moral implications from the actions of the chief personages related to the passion narrative. For instance, only

---

[1] M 92, p. 210.   [2] M 91, p. 207.   [3] C 2, 23–4, pp. 152–3.

[4] But cf. Heb. 5.7: "in the days of his flesh, he offered up prayers and supplications, with loud cries and tears, to him who was able to save him from death".

[5] C 2, 25, p. 155; M 92, p. 209.

Matthew (26.22) and Mark (14.19) represent the disciples as asking about the betrayer, "Is it I?" These evangelists, "being men", were mentioning the fact of the changeable will of those who are still making progress.[1] Judas is the prime example of the man who has such a changeable will. There were contrary feelings in his heart,[2] and his later repentance proves their existence.[3] Caiaphas is obviously evil. Matthew explicitly mentions him (26.3,57); Luke mentions not only Satan and Judas but also the high priests (22.3–4); and similarly Mark mentions Judas (14.10) and the hostile high priest as well (14.60–3). Origen is placing the responsibility for the crucifixion on Caiaphas.[4] Herod was partly responsible for Jesus' death, for he could have released him and prevented his death;[5] Herod's wife too may have plotted against Jesus, as she did against John the Baptist[6] On the other hand, Pilate was not responsible at all. His attitude toward Jesus was favourable, and he recognized him as the real king of the Jews;[7] indeed, he recognized him as the Christ,[8] though he was not actually an "eyewitness of the Logos".[9]

THE CRUCIFIXION

In 1 Cor. 1.23 the apostle Paul states that the apostolic preaching of Christ crucified was a stumbling-block to Jews and folly to gentiles. To a considerable extent the exegesis of Origen represents an attempt to remove these difficulties from the accounts of the crucifixion. Gnostic teachers had already argued that the spiritual Christ could not really have been crucified. Origen comes very close to their view when he explains to Celsus that no Christian really believes that the Life could have died; it was the human Jesus who was crucified.[10] In the synoptic gospels he reads that Simon of Cyrene carried Jesus' cross (Matt. 27.32; Mark 15.21; Luke 23.26); but in John 19.17 the cross is carried by Jesus himself. He gives two explanations of this difference. First he

[1] J 32, 19, p. 459.   [2] C 2, 11, pp. 138–9.
[3] J 32, 19, p. 458; M 117, pp. 246–7. Other citations in Bauer, op cit., p. 174. The other disciples fled because they had not made enough progress; ibid., pp. 179–80.
[4] J 28, 13–14, pp. 405–8.   [5] M 10, 21, pp. 28–9.   [6] M 13, 2, p. 185.
[7] M 118–19, pp. 251–2.   [8] M 124, p. 258.   [9] Cf. Bertrand, op. cit., p. 25.
[10] C 7, 16, p. 168.

points out that John is speaking of the spiritual nature of Jesus; in relation to this nature Jesus carried his own cross. He is unwilling to give up the lesson taught by the synoptics, however; they show that we should carry the cross too;[1] and therefore he suggests that perhaps Simon and Jesus took turns in carrying the cross. Perhaps, as some say, Simon means "obedience".[2]

Another difficulty occurs in the story of the two thieves crucified with Jesus. According to all four gospels Jesus was crucified between them (Matt. 27.38; Mark 15.27; Luke 23.33; John 19.18). Nothing more is said of them in John, but according to Matthew and Mark both of them reviled him (Matt. 27.44; Mark 15.32), while in Luke 23.39–43 one reviled him while the other was penitent. Origen does not usually favour Luke against the other evangelists, but here he suggests that Luke, "as he announced (1.3), is giving a more accurate account". One thief was converted because he had heard of Jesus' miracles or saw the darkness which was "already" present according to Luke 23.44. On the other hand, Origen is unwilling to abandon entirely an explanation he has provided in the *Commentary on John* (in a part now lost). There he has suggested that there were really four thieves, the two of Matthew and Mark and the two of Luke.[3]

According to Luke 23.43 Jesus said to the penitent thief, "To-day you will be with me in Paradise." Since in the Church's view Jesus did not go immediately to Paradise but descended "to the so-called heart of the earth", the text presented a difficulty. As Origen states, some critics proceeded to remove the verse, treating it as an interpolation.[4] He prefers a simpler explanation: Jesus set the believing thief in Paradise before descending.[5] In any event, the words contain a deeper meaning. "To-day" refers not to an earthly day but to the whole new age now beginning.[6]

In describing the darkness "over the whole earth" or "over the whole land" from the sixth to the ninth hour (Matt. 27.45; Mark 15.33), Luke (23.44–5) added the words "while the sun's light failed" or "while the sun was eclipsed" (τοῦ ἡλίου

---

[1] Cf. also *M* 12, 24, p. 125.   [2] *M* 126, pp. 262–4.
[3] *M* 133, pp. 270–1. Marcion omitted the story of the penitent thief.
[4] Marcion deleted not only this verse but the whole pericope.
[5] *L* fr. 81, p. 273.   [6] *J* 32, 32, pp. 479–80.

ἐκλιπόντος; according to some manuscripts, "and the sun was darkened", καὶ ἐσκοτίσθη ὁ ἥλιος). A certain historian named Thallus identified the darkness with an eclipse, but Julius Africanus pointed out that since an eclipse was impossible at the time of the full moon (Passover), the darkness must have been "made by God".[1] Origen follows a similar line of reasoning. He knows that the anecdotal historian Phlegon has mentioned an eclipse in the reign of Tiberius—though not at the time of the full moon,[2] when an eclipse would be impossible. He proceeds to show that neither Matthew nor Mark mentions an eclipse, and that it is absent from most manuscripts of Luke.[3] How did it get into the text? Perhaps it was due to a mistaken conjecture by someone who wanted to explain the darkness; more probably it was inserted by enemies of the Church. In any case, it is an unnecessary addition, for the "darkness" mentioned by Matthew is clearly limited to Jerusalem or to Judaea, since the events described in what follows (Matt. 27.51-3) are related to those places. The darkness was probably due to very dark clouds.[4]

Another difficulty was to be found in Matt. 27.46 (Mark 15.34; no parallels in Luke or John), where Jesus cries out, "My God, my God, why hast thou forsaken me?" It might be supposed—as it is by most New Testament critics—that this cry of dereliction expresses the fullness of the human suffering of Jesus. Origen is anxious to avoid this interpretation, and he therefore insists that when Matthew and Mark speak of a "loud" or "great" voice, they are referring to the "divine voice" by which the cry was uttered.[5]

The sequence of the events accompanying the death of Jesus is given differently by the three synoptists. Matthew describes an earthquake and the opening of tombs; a centurion and others,

---

[1] M. J. Routh, *Reliquiae Sacrae* II (2nd ed., Oxford, 1846), pp. 297–8.

[2] Perhaps the solar eclipse of 24, Nov. 29, or the lunar eclipse of 3, Apr. 33 (P. de Labriolle, *La réaction païenne*, Paris, 1934, p. 218). In writing against Celsus, Origen is not so critical: see p. 75.

[3] Sun darkened, K θ, many others, Latin, Syriac, Marcion; sun eclipsed, B S C.

[4] *M* 134, pp. 272–5.

[5] *M* 135, p. 280. In *C* 3, 32 (p. 229) Origen simply refers this verse to Jesus' power to lay down his life. For the idea that a divine voice should be unique cf. Celsus in *C* 6, 75, p. 144.

seeing the miracles, acknowledge Jesus as the Son of God (Matt. 27.51–4). Mark has none of the miracles; the centurion's confession is based on the way in which Jesus died (Mark 15.44–5). In Luke 23.47 the centurion speaks of him as a "righteous" or "innocent" man. Origen is not much impressed by the story in Matthew, which refers to the "fear" of the witnesses and makes their faith depend on miracles. He finds more meaningful the account in Mark, where the centurion understood the events in proportion to his ability to understand (for Origen the κεντυρίων of Mark was different from the ἑκατοντάρχης of Matthew and Luke). He understood the real miracle, which was the quick death of Jesus, the one who had power to lay down his life.[1]

THE TEACHING OF JESUS

From the opening chapters of the four gospels, Origen was aware that there was almost as much diversity in their accounts of the teaching of John the Baptist and of Jesus as there was in their stories of Jesus' ministry. He usually treats this kind of diversity, however, as complementary rather than contradictory. The different evangelists, inspired by the Spirit, draw different lessons from what John or Jesus taught. For example, the four evangelists say that John came to baptize in water; only Matthew (3.11) added "for repentance" or "with repentance in view". He was teaching that the utility of baptism depends on the predisposition of the person who is baptized.[2] But when Origen encounters the word "repent" again, in Matthew's account of the proclamation of Jesus (4.17), he notes that it has already been spoken by John the Baptist (Matt. 3.2) and that it is lacking at this point in some manuscripts.[3] He therefore deletes it and says that since Jesus was receiving "a people prepared" (Luke 1.17) and no longer in need of repentance, he did not urge them to repent.[4] When he deals with the aphoristic, "gnomic" teaching of

---

[1] John 10.18; *M* 140, pp. 290–1.   [2] *J* 6, 33, p. 142.

[3] The word is omitted in the old Latin k, in the Sinaitic and Curetonian Syriac, and by Clement and Eusebius.

[4] *M* fr. 74, p. 45.

Jesus in the synoptic gospels, he cannot believe that it is as simple as it appears to be. Thus in the treatise *De principiis* he cites synoptic sayings as examples of irrational or impossible commands. "Carry no purse, no bag, no sandals; and salute no one on the road" (Luke 10.4). "If anyone strikes you on the right cheek, turn to him the other also" (Matt. 5.39; you would be struck on the left cheek, not the right!). "If your right eye causes you to sin, pluck it out and throw it away" (Matt. 5.29; how could you tell which eye was responsible?). These commandments cannot be taken literally.[1]

As we have already seen, early Christians were accustomed to classify the gospels as ἀπομνημονεύματα which contained χρεῖαι and γνῶμαι. Origen is no exception to this rule; he uses the verb ἀπομνημονεύειν in speaking of the work of the evangelists.[2] Moreover, when the elder John dealt with the χρεῖαι contained in Mark, he made use of conventional rhetorical analysis of such materials. It is on the foundation laid by his predecessors in gospel criticism and in Graeco-Roman rhetoric that Origen builds when he discusses the teachings handed down from Jesus. Among rhetoricians the χρεία could be criticized on the grounds that it was obscure, that it added unnecessary details or omitted what was necessary, that it was impossible, that it was improbable or incredible, that it was false, that it was prejudicial, that it was useless, or that it was shameful.[3] Similar criticisms could be made of legislation.[4] And on either basis Origen could analyse the teaching of Jesus as reported in the synoptics, and could declare it "irrational" or "impossible". The teaching of Jesus could thus be analysed from a rhetorical point of view; so could the prayer which he taught his disciples.

The rhetorician Theon provided an elaborate classification of different kinds of χρεῖαι (97.11—101.2), and in dealing with the Lord's Prayer Origen seems to be making use of something like it. Theon divides his "verbal χρεῖαι" into two kinds, those which are declarative (ἀποφαντικόν) and those which are responsive (ἀποκρίτικον). One kind of responsive verbal χρεία is that given

---

[1] *P* 4, 3, 3, pp. 327–8. Cf. *M* 13, 24, p. 244. [2] See the Glossary, p. 120.
[3] Theon, p. 104, 15–18 (examples, 104.18—105.18). [4] *P.* 129, 7–10.

in answer to a request (κατὰ πύσμα) which requires a relatively
long answer. It would appear that Origen has something like this
in mind when he analyses the Lord's Prayer as reported by Matthew (6.9–13) and by Luke (11.2–4). He lists three possible
explanations of the differences. (1) The prayer might be the same;
but according to Matthew it was delivered on a mountain and
without a prior request, while in Luke it was set forth "in a
certain place" after a request had been made. (2) The prayer
might be the same, expressed on two different occasions. (3)
Perhaps there were two different, but partly similar, prayers,
delivered on different occasions.[1]

Origen obviously rejects the first two solutions because of the
differences between the prayers and their circumstances.[2] By
looking at the circumstances he is able to bring the prayers into
some relationship with Greek rhetoric. He therefore explains
that the prayer in Matthew was given "without any previous
request, in a declarative manner", or "in a declarative discourse".[3]
This statement seems to imply that for Origen the Matthaean
version is a declarative verbal χρεία uttered in circumstances not
clearly defined (cf. Theon 97.16–22), while the Lucan version is
of the kind given in answer to a request. Because the prayers have
to be given different formal classifications they cannot be simply
identified, even though Origen is willing to consider the possibility that the Lucan form is an abbreviation of that found in
Matthew. His own solution, expressed in a fragment on Luke, is
that there are two prayers which contain some common materials.[4]

Naturally Origen considers the detailed differences. Matthew
uses the invocation, "Our Father in the heavens", since "in the
heavens" is frequently found in his gospel; on the other hand, by
omitting the expression Luke shows that "the divine" is trans-
cendent.[5] "Hallowed be thy name" is imperative in form, but

[1] O 18, 3, pp. 341–1.
[2] Cf. E. G. Jay, *Origen's Treatise on Prayer* (London, 1954), p. 138 n1.
[3] I translate "declarative" from ἀποφαντικός, my own emendation (based on Theon) of the manuscript's ἀποτακτικός, which does not make sense. Jay (op. cit., p. 137 n3) emends, following Bentley and Delarue, to ἀποτατικός; he then translates "in an ex-tended manner" and "in an extended discourse".
[4] L fr. 41, p. 253; cf. O 30, 1, p. 393 (Luke's version esoteric, Matthew's exoteric).
[5] L fr. 42. p. 253; cf. O 23, 1, pp. 349–50.

optative in meaning, just as in the Greek of the Septuagint.[1] As for ἐπιούσιος (translated "daily" in English versions), Origen is eager to show that it cannot be used of ordinary bread of any kind. It is a word not found in Greek, either among "the wise" or among the unlearned. This statement suggests that Origen has been unable to find it in the lexicons in use at Alexandria or Caesarea in his time. He thinks that it was probably made up by the evangelists; in the Septuagint too there are examples of peculiar Greek words or forms. And he proceeds to derive it from ἐπί "upon" in the sense of "beyond", and οὐσία, "being" in the sense of "actuality" or "perceptibility to sense". This analysis,[2] as Cadiou has observed, is in large measure based on research in lexicons.[3] "Deliver us from evil" or "the evil one" is omitted in the Lucan version because Jesus is giving private instruction to his disciples who had already been delivered. Matthew's prayer, then, is for public use; that in Luke, for theologically-minded Christians.[4]

When Origen turned from prayers to parables he found himself on firmer rhetorical ground. As we have already seen, he sometimes used "parable" to include anything which a rhetorician might have classified as "fiction". But he was of course aware that the parables of Jesus were more than ordinary fictions; they were fictions which contained a special point, "metaphorically" indicated "by transference".[5] Rhetoricians gave similar definitions. Herodian tells us that a "parable" is a comparison with something which happens or is like what happens,[6] and Trypho's doctrine is similar.[7]

Now Origen knew that in the synoptic gospels there are many parables told by Jesus. Mark provides a collection of them in his fourth chapter, and he also explains why they were used and gives an allegorical explanation of one of them. "With many such parables he spoke the word to them, as they were able to bear it; but apart from parables he did not speak to them, and privately

---

[1] O 24, 5, pp. 355–6.   [2] O 27, 7–8, pp. 366–8.

[3] R. Cadiou in *Revue des études grecques* 45 (1932), pp. 275–6; actually on one lexicon, the doxography edited by H. Diels (*Doxographi Graeci*, Berlin, 1879 and 1929, pp. 457–8) in its Stobaean form.

[4] *L* fr. 42, p. 254.   [5] Lommatzsch 13, 220, 226.

[6] III, 104, 1 Spengel.   [7] III, 201, 12.

he explained everything to his own disciples" (Mark 4.33–4). Both Matthew and Luke closely followed Mark, though both omitted the notion of secret explanation, perhaps because it was being exploited by heterodox opponents.

Origen was delighted with the Marcan theory of private explanation. "One must consider, in regard to every parable whose explanation (διήγησις) is not recorded by the evangelists, that he explained everything to his own disciples in private, and therefore those who wrote the gospels concealed the interpretation (σαφήνεια) of the parables, since the matters revealed in them were greater than the nature of writing, and the world itself could not contain the books written (John 21.25) on such parables."[1] Therefore the private teaching of Jesus to his disciples (Mark 4.34) has not been recorded,[2] and Origen can say that "we confess that we do not reach the full depth of the meaning of the parables".[3]

There are those who suppose that the gospel writings have only one meaning, but actually God's plan provided that they should be understood simply by the simple. For those who have the desire and the ability to hear them more acutely, there lie concealed wise matters, worthy of the Word of God.[4]

To Mark's collection of parables, Matthew added the parable of the tares (Matt. 13.24–30) and an explanation of it (13.36–43), given by Jesus when he had left the crowds and had gone into "the house". Origen took advantage of this expression to compare other gospel passages in which the "house of Jesus" was mentioned, and he reached the conclusion that it has a symbolical meaning.[5] "To approach Jesus in his house is to be introduced to a higher revelation and to close intimacy with the Son of God."[6]

For this reason a careful allegorical interpretation of the parables is not only defensible but necessary. In the parable of the sower all three evangelists wrote that some of the seed fell "by the way"; they did not write "in the way" because according to John 14.6 Jesus himself is "the way". But Matthew and Mark

---

[1] *M* 14, 12, p. 304.   [2] *C* 6, 6, p. 76.   [3] *M* p. 305.
[4] *M* 10, 1, p. 2.   [5] *M* 10, 1, pp. 1–2.
[6] F. Bertrand, *Mystique de Jésus chez Origène* (Paris, 1951), p. 81.

paid more attention to symbolism than Luke did. They wrote that some of the seed fell "on rocky ground", while Luke wrote "on the rock". He should not have done so, since either Christ or Peter was the rock.[1] In the explanation of this parable, Matthew mentioned "the evil one", Mark "Satan", and Luke "the devil". Origen points out the fact, but his explanation has not been preserved; presumably he identified the three. Some hearers receive the Word "immediately" with joy, but have no root in themselves. Luke omits the word "immediately" but it is necessary in order to define the class of believers being described.[2] Finally, both Matthew and Mark speak of the falling away of these believers in "tribulation or persecution"; Luke mentions only "temptation" or "trial"—he is generalizing.[3]

Here we have an explanation of an explanation. Origen adheres fairly closely to the literal meaning of the text. But he cannot refrain from trying to create a rather systematic interpretation of Jesus' use of parables, especially in the light of Mark's remarks about the privacy of the true exegesis. Parables are for outsiders, or for disciples who will later be given private instruction.[4] But according to Matthew (13.44–50) Jesus addressed three parables, those about the treasure, the pearl, and the net, to his disciples in the house. Origen's explanation of this difficulty is based on rhetorical analysis. These three parables are not parables but comparisons (ὁμοιώσεις). When Mark 4.30 has Jesus say, "With what can we compare the kingdom of God, or what parable shall we use for it?" the difference between a comparison and a parable is indicated (*M* 10, 4, pp. 4–5).[5]

Not all rhetoricians differentiated these forms in just this way. For example, Trypho treats the comparison (simile) as the genus which includes three species, one of them being the "parable".[6] On the other hand, Herodian agrees with Origen that a parable and a simile are different. A simile is shorter than a parable and does not end with a general conclusion.[7]

---

[1] *M* fr. 291, pp. 129–30. [2] *M* fr. 293, p. 131. [3] *M* fr. 292, p. 130.

[4] *L* fr. 26, p. 245. [5] Actually it is not indicated; this is Semitic parallelism.

[6] III, 200, 4–6 Spengel; so also Polybius of Sardis, III, 106, 16–18; and (more elaborately) Cocondrius, III, 239, 25–9.

[7] III, 104, 1–7. The three Matthaean parables which Origen treats as similes have no conclusions.

Therefore Origen did have good rhetorical precedent for his analysis. The only difficulty with it is that the distinction he makes does not seem to have occurred to the evangelist whose work he is discussing.

The evangelist Matthew (13.53) refers back to the whole preceding section and says that "when Jesus had finished these parables, he went away from there". It would appear that the inspired Matthew did not understand the distinction Origen has been making. All is not lost, however, for the allegorist. When Jesus went away, he came to his own country (Matt. 13.54). Therefore he was not in his own country at the time he was speaking in parables. His disciples had to follow him to his own country—literally Nazareth or Bethlehem, mystically Judaea.[1] Since they were in an alien land, he spoke to them in parables, says Origen. We might ask how, if they were in an alien land, they could be in "the house of Jesus". The allegorical explanation does not fit the text it is supposed to explain. Origen would have been better advised had he abandoned the notion that parables were addressed only to outsiders.

In any event, he feels free to interpret the parables as allegories, and in explaining the deeper meaning of the parable of the unmerciful servant (Matt. 18.23–35) he explicitly says that he is doing so in a manner analogous to that of the explanations given by the evangelists.[2] The expositor needs the spirit of Christ in producing his exegesis,[3] for the only real exegete of the parables is Jesus, who privately explained everything to his own disciples.[4] For this reason, heretical exegetes, who find the wrathful Demiurge in the parable, are wrong—though in Origen's view the "tormentors" are those (presumably angels) in charge of punishments,[5] and the "accounting" which takes place in the parable refers to the Last Judgement. This point is confirmed by exegesis of other synoptic parables, and we find it strikingly paralleled in gnostic (Carpocratian) interpretations of similar passages.[6]

[1] M 10, 16, pp. 20–1. On the necessity for leaving alien lands to come to Jesus cf. Bertrand, op. cit., pp. 72–4.
[2] M 14, 6, p. 287   [3] P. 288.   [4] M 14, 11, p. 302.
[5] 14, 13, p. 313.
[6] 14, 12, pp. 305–8. Irenaeus, *Adv. haer.* 1, 25, 4, pp. 208–9. Cf. also L 23, pp. 154–5.

In dealing with this parable Origen comes close to providing a systematic treatment of it. First he gives a moral application of it; he calls this the περίνοια. Then he mentions the fact that there is a simpler and more literal meaning. But he is eager to press onward to the higher and more mystical explanation, analogous to the explanations given by the evangelists themselves.[1] He has no real exegetical system, however. When he comes to the parable of the labourers in the vineyard (Matt. 20.1–16), he gives four different explanations. First comes an allegorical explanation like that of the parable of the Good Samaritan, with which we shall presently deal. Second, the five groups of labourers are identified with five stages of the spiritual life, related to five spiritual senses. Third, the parable contains a secret doctrine relating to the creation of the soul. And finally, Origen provides simpler, "more useful" exegesis for those who are shocked by the more secret doctrines.[2] As Daniélou has pointed out, this treatment is gnostic in tendency and (partly) in content.[3]

The parable of the Good Samaritan in Luke (10.29–37) had already been taken allegorically by Origen's predecessors.[4] For them the man in the story was Adam, who went down from paradise (Jerusalem) to the world (Jericho) and was mistreated by hostile powers (robbers). The law (the priest) and the prophets (the Levite) passed him by, but Christ (the Samaritan) cured his disobedience (his wounds) and set him on his own body (the beast) and brought him to the church (the inn)—and so on. Origen accepts this exegesis, simply adding refinements of his own. The man is not only Adam but also Jesus; the Samaritan is the Son of God.[5] Similarly the parable of the Prodigal Son has an allegorical meaning, for the repentant youth says, "I have sinned against heaven and before thee" (Luke 15.21). He could not have said "against heaven" had heaven not been his native country.[6]

Origen was not favourably impressed by the efforts of others

[1] 14, 6. pp. 286–7.
[2] 15, 32–37, pp. 446–61. For "secret doctrines" cf. P 4, 2, 8, p. 320, etc.
[3] Origène, pp. 196–8.
[4] Irenaeus, Adv. haer. 3, 17, 3, p. 93.
[5] L 34, pp. 201–2. For the Samaritan as Saviour cf. J 20, 35, p. 374, and Daniélou, op. cit., p. 195; so Clement, Quis div. salv.? 29, 2.
[6] L fr. 72, p. 269.

to provide equally subtle analysis. Some critic wanted to reject the parable of Dives and Lazarus. He argued that if Lazarus lay in Abraham's bosom (Luke 16.22–3), others must have lain there earlier. When another righteous man came to the place, Lazarus would have to be removed to make room for him. Origen points out that this critic was not aware that "myriads" could be in Abraham's bosom at the same time. After all, in the gospel of John we read that John "historically" lay in Jesus' bosom; but the Son of God was in the bosom of the Father.[1]

Given the allegorical meaning of parables, it was obvious that difficult sayings of Jesus had to be interpreted allegorically too. According to Matt. 18.2–3, Jesus set a child in the midst of the disciples and said, "Truly I say to you, unless you turn and become like children, you will not enter into the kingdom of heaven". Why "like children"? Origen explains that infants (παιδία) do not possess any of the passions, including fear; therefore to be like children means being free from emotion.[2] This is his "simpler" explanation, but he can give another, "either for the sake of doctrine or for the sake of exegetical exercise" (εἴτε ὡς δόγματος εἴτε ὡς γυμνασίου ἕνεκεν). According to this interpretation the child is the Holy Spirit, which Jesus placed in the midst of his disciples, and we should be like the apostles![3]

Another difficult saying of Jesus is found in Matt. 19.12, which speaks of three classes of eunuchs: (1) "from their mother's womb"; (2) made so by men; and (3) self-made on account of the kingdom of heaven. Origen divides exegetes of this verse into two groups. The first group takes the first two classes of eunuchs literally and "corporeally", treats the third class as analogues, and proceeds to act upon this exegesis. These people are "friends of the gospel letter" and they "do not understand that Jesus also spoke of these matters in parables and that they were said in spirit". They cite the Sentences of Sextus in defence of their view, and quote Philo at his most literal-minded point.[4]

---

[1] J 32, 20, p. 462; L fr. 77, p. 271. For the symbolical meaning cf. Bertrand, op. cit., pp. 36–7; 137–9.

[2] M 13, 16, p. 221.   [3] 13, 18, pp. 226–7.

[4] M 15, 1, pp. 348–50; 15, 3, p. 354. *Quod det. pot. insid. soleat* 176, cf. H. Chadwick, *The Sentences of Sextus* (Cambridge, 1959), pp. 109–12.

The second group, including Origen himself, recognizes that the first two classes are "somatic" but that the third is not.[1]

Similarly in expounding verses in Luke Origen treats them as allegorical. "Let the dead bury their own dead" (Luke 9.60) is mystical because it cannot be taken literally.[2] "Greet no one by the way" (Luke 10.4) is clearly irrational if taken as a literal command.[3] The saying about five sparrows in Luke 12.6 is like and unlike the saying about two sparrows in Matthew, they can be referred to the five spiritual senses of the righteous.[4] Jesus' counsel not to invite friends to a banquet (Luke 14.12) cannot be meant literally, "for it is not characteristic of a wise man to invite the poor who are not believers, or not to invite his friends who are poor and believers".[5]

The method is always the same. If a saying, taken in a crudely literal way, seems impossible or irrational, the exegete is free to treat it in an allegorical, "mystical" way and use this treatment as part of his theological construction.

ESCHATOLOGICAL ELEMENTS

Since in Origen's view the most profound of the gospels was that according to John, and since in John the eschatological emphasis of the synoptic gospels is largely lacking, it is not surprising that he was concerned with the reinterpretation of eschatology. He knows that it is present in the synoptics. But "those who hear the gospel more deeply, and do everything they can so that the gospel may not be veiled in any part of it, do not pay much attention (*non multum curant*) to the universal end of the age and the question whether it will be sudden and universal or by degrees; they pay attention only to this point, that the end of each individual takes place when he does not know the day or the hour of his departure, and that upon each one of us 'the day of the Lord will come like a thief' " (1 Thess. 5.2). So when Mark 13.35 speaks

[1] On the exegesis of this verse cf. W. Bauer in *Neutestamentliche Studien G. Heinrici* (Leipzig, 1914), pp. 235–44. The saying about plucking out an eye or cutting off a hand (Matt. 5.29–30) must also be understood allegorically (*P* 4, 3, 3, p. 328; *M* 13, 24, p. 244; 15, 2, p. 353).

[2] *L* fr. 29, p. 246. [3] *P* 4, 3, 3, p. 327; *M* 15, 2, p. 352.
[4] *L* fr. 57, p. 260. [5] *L* fr. 68, p. 266.

of the master's coming "in the evening, or at midnight, or at cockcrow, or in the morning", Origen explains that these moments refer to youth, middle age, more advanced age, and old age.[1]

What then of such sayings as Matt. 19.29, which seems to say that believers will receive a hundredfold the houses, brothers, sisters, father, mother, children, and lands they have left for Jesus' name's sake? Origen says that the literal meaning of this verse is "not despicable"; believers actually are hated by their relatives and receive innumerable spiritual gifts. They gain Christian brothers and sisters, Christian parents who are the bishops and the presbyters, and Christian children who are the children in the Church. But "lands" and "houses" cannot be taken literally except by a "forced" interpretation. And if they are allegorical, then the other items must also be allegorical. The "brothers and sisters" must be angels as well as human beings; the "lands and houses" are to be found in the divine paradise and in the city of God.[2]

When the mother of the sons of Zebedee (Matt. 20.20) or the sons themselves (Mark 10.35) ask for seats beside Jesus in his glory, they are expressing a false corporeal understanding. If the mother asks, her request reflects "womanish simplicity"; if they ask, they are "men who are still imperfect and know nothing".[3]

The language of the "little apocalypse", therefore, must obviously be taken allegorically. For example, it says in Matt. 24.29 that "the sun will be darkened, and the moon will not give its light". No doubt such darkness can be explained as due to smoke from a cosmic conflagration. But the world will not come to an end in this manner; instead, we read in the same verse of Matthew that "the stars will fall from heaven". Moreover, taken literally the verse contradicts Isa. 30.26, which speaks of the light of the moon being as the light of the sun, and the light of the sun being "sevenfold". Origen knows literalists who may say that something "by nature impossible" is possible, but his own conclusion is that the darkened sun is the devil, while the moon is the congregation of the wicked, and the stars are hostile powers in

[1] *M* 56, p. 130. [2] *M* 15, 25, pp. 422–5. [3] *M* 16, 4, p. 473.

heaven.[1] Therefore the "clouds" on which the Son of Man will come (Matt. 24.30) must be "animate and rational clouds".[2] Matt. 24.31 says that the angels will gather the elect "from one end of heaven to the other"; but Mark 13.27 mentions the gathering "from the end of the earth to the end of the heaven". This disagreement proves that both expressions are allegorical.[3]

What Origen feels about all this eschatological material is clearly shown in his comment on Matt. 25.34, where the evangelist speaks of "the foundation (καταβολή) of the world". There is a deeper meaning to this expression (etymologically it could be related to "casting down"), but Origen says he will not entrust it to writing. To do so would be like casting pearls before swine![4] In the early treatise *De principiis* he was not so reticent. There he said that it referred to the descent of souls into the world.[5]

In other words, behind the simple and inadequate literal meaning of eschatological sayings in the gospels there lies a deep hidden mystery, one which has meaning not only in relation to the future of individuals but also in relation to Origen's own mythological understanding of the origin of the souls and of the world.

One might suppose that the saying, "There are some standing here who will not taste death before they see the Son of Man coming in his kingdom" (Matt. 16.28), would present some difficulties. But Origen is able to face them. We have already seen that in dealing with the question of the perpetual virginity of Mary, seemingly contradicted in Matt. 1.25, he insists that in scripture the words for "before" (ἕως οὗ, or ἕως ἄν) do not necessarily set a limit for the action described. So here he makes the same point, comparing Matt. 28.20; "I am with you always, before (ἕως) the end of the age." No limit is set in either case.[6] But since the problem of dying remains, he then goes on to explain that to "taste death" does not literally mean to die.[7] Here his exegesis seems no more reliable than it often is.

[1] *M* 48–9, pp. 99–103.   [2] *M* 50, p. 109. So also on I Thess. 4.17 (*PG* 14, 1302D).
[3] *M* 51, p. 115.   [4] *M* 71, p. 168.
[5] 3, 5, 4, pp. 273–5 (citing Matt. 25.34; John 17.24; Eph. 1.4; and Heb. 4.3); cf. *J* 19, 22 (p. 324).
[6] *M* 12, 34, pp. 146–7.   [7] *M* 12, 35, pp. 149–50; cf. *J* 20, 43, p. 386.

It is significant that when Origen is dealing with an eschatological passage in Matthew he reveals the nature of his method. In Matt. 19.27 Peter says to Jesus, "Lo, we have left everything and followed you; what then shall we have?" Origen cannot believe that even Peter could have asked a question so crudely literal in appearance. "One reader will retain these words in accordance with the literal meaning, but another, having refuted them (ἀνασκευάσας), will allegorize the content of the letter because of its insignificance."[1] Once more the method of ἀνασκευή is to be applied at a point where the literal meaning is offensive to a symbolist. By making use of it, the teaching of Jesus and the apostles can be freed from its eschatological framework, and the true spiritual content can be restored.

[1] hos ou megalophues, M 15, 21, p. 409.

5

THE ENIGMA OF JESUS

As Frédéric Bertrand points out, in his valuable *Mystique de Jésus* to which we have already referred one of Origen's principal concerns was to "internalize" Jesus.[1] Sometimes Origen retains the historical letter of the gospels; sometimes he does not; but always he is concerned with the inner, spiritual meaning of the text. And it is in relation to the life of Jesus that he develops a whole system of symbolism, and refers it to the Christian's spiritual development.

> What the evangelists report is oriented toward a reality of a profound and mysterious order. All the external facts which they described portray the inner life of the Christian and of the Church. In other words, it is in the soul of the believer and in the Church that the mysteries denoted in these pages are now reproduced.[2]

This fact means that the rôle of literary and historical criticism, important though it is, is always subsidiary to Origen's main concern with the soul.

Yet it is obvious that Origen did make use of the techniques of criticism and that at significant points they indicated to him the direction of his thought. Along with his conception of development in the spiritual life of the believer he held a conception of development in the life and thought of the apostles; it was John who, because he reclined on the Lord's bosom, most fully understood his divine nature. Therefore when comparison with the other gospels shows that John disagrees with them, one must believe that the disagreement is intentional and that the spiritual meaning is that set forth by John.

This kind of analysis is most fully utilized in the books of the *Commentary on John* written soon after Origen's departure from Alexandria for Caesarea; but it recurs in books which he wrote at a much later date. He never abandoned it, even though over a period of time he came to value more highly the historical

---

[1] *Mystique de Jésus chez Origène* (Paris, 1951), p. 146.   [2] Ibid., p. 41.

elements in all four gospels. In general, however, he did not value them simply because they were historical but because he realized that they had meaning for the edification of simpler believers and because they could be used as stepping stones toward symbolism.

What lies behind Origen's understanding of the gospels, and indeed of the Christian religion, in this manner? We should surely agree with Bertrand that to a considerable extent Origen is building upon his own religious experience.[1] But the reality of this experience is not denied if one goes rather more deeply into both the personal and the philosophical roots of Origen's "pedagogical idealism" and recognizes with Hal Koch the close ties between Origen's thought and that of some of his contemporaries.[2] In Origen's view of the inspiration of various biblical writers there is a strong emphasis on the pedagogical work of the Logos. We have already seen that he believed that Paul made progress toward perfection, and that the greatest of the evangelists was John, who reclined on the Lord's bosom. But he was willing to express the view even more plainly, as he does in the *Selecta in Ieremiam*: Paul laid the foundation, while Luke and Timothy built the upper story.[3] The illumination possessed by Timothy, however, was inferior to that of Paul.[4] In Origen's opinion the universe was a great school room. The Logos was the master of the school; he appeared in various guises to various pupils. His best pupils were the apostles, but best of all were the apostles Paul and John.[5]

It is easy enough to see that a scheme like this is closely related to Greek philosophical conceptions of Origen's time. Koch has traced the parallels in considerable detail. We should add that it corresponds with the course of education provided in the Greek philosophical school. The curriculum of God is remarkably

---

[1] Ibid., pp. 148–52; cf. also the work he cites, W. Völker, *Das Vollkommenheitsideal des Origenes* (Tübingen, 1931).

[2] *Pronoia und Paideusis: Studien über Origenes und sein Verhältnis zum Platonismus* (Berlin-Leipzig, 1932).

[3] Lommatzsch 15, 445; A. Zöllig, *Die Inspirationslehre des Origenes* (Freiburg, 1903), pp. 73–6.

[4] *M* 12, 15, p. 104.   [5] *C* 3, 76, p. 268.

similar to the curriculum with which Origen himself had been acquainted. Brought up at first with encyclical studies such as grammar and rhetoric, he passed through and beyond these to philosophy and the exegesis of scripture. He came to realize that the study of literature, in which for him history was apparently included, was merely preliminary to the true philosophy which lay in and behind the words of scripture. As we have repeatedly seen, he did not abandon the study of rhetoric. At any rate, he did not stop using its methods. But he used them in the service of philosophical theology.

Does Origen's idea of revelation as education come altogether from his own experience and his own education? We must allow for the influence of another factor in his thought. This factor is based on the data he possessed about the development of Pauline spirituality as reflected in the epistles. But he was also aware that the other apostles advanced in their apprehension of the meaning of Christ, and that they proclaimed a more perfect doctrine after the resurrection.[1] Peter's early rebuke of Jesus shows how little he understood.[2] Neither Peter nor any other apostle was perfect before the Passion.[3]

Now since in Origen's opinion the true meaning of Jesus' teaching was not eschatological, he encountered a difficulty when he found John the son of Zebedee, traditionally the author of the "spiritual" gospel, asking for a seat at Jesus' side in his kingdom (Mark 10.35). Two explanations were possible. Either John did not write the fourth gospel (but Origen had no reason to question the tradition that he did) or else his understanding of Jesus' teaching was considerably modified by later events. Origen took the latter alternative and stated that at this point John and his brother were "still imperfect and completely ignorant".[4]

In other words, the theory of development was made necessary by a combination of evidence from the gospels and evidence from tradition about the evangelists. The consequence of the theory must be, though Origen does not explicitly say so, that John has radically rewritten the life of Jesus from the standpoint of his later

[1] M 12, 15, p. 108, 12, 18, pp. 109–10.   [2] M 12, 21, p. 116. Cf. M 13, 9, p. 206.
[3] M 12, 40, p. 158.   [4] M 16, 4, p. 473.

knowledge while the other three evangelists have often been content to relate historical facts. Origen really does state this consequence, though in different language, when he says that John emphasized the divine nature of Jesus while the other evangelists laid stress on his humanity. This is to say that the gospels disagree because John wrote a theological treatise unlike the less explicitly theological synoptics.

So much for the general theory of development. What of the specific differences to be found in the gospels? Here we have found a remarkable use of the rhetorical method of ἀνασκευή, which constantly comes to light all the way from the early treatise De principiis to the late Commentary on Matthew. In the late apologetic treatise Contra Celsum Origen puts ἀνασκευή in reverse and tries to prove the historical reliability of some of the gospel narratives, but he himself admits the difficulty of his new task. His results are rather less convincing than those reached in a more negative direction. His heart does not seem to be in his work, for the confirmation of historicity does not lead to the immediate possibility of allegorizing.

Perhaps it should be said that he is really interested not in history as such but in the use of historical methods. Even with all his insistence—some of the time—that the events described in the Bible really occurred, "certain passages", as H.-C. Puech has observed, "remain alarming".[1] Puech cites J 10, 18 (p. 189):

> You must not suppose that historical realities are figures for other historical realities and corporeal things for other corporeal realities; instead, corporeal things are figures for spiritual realities and historical realities for intelligible realities.

If Origen really means what he says, he is definitely abandoning typology in favour of allegory and emptying events of their historical meaning.[2]

The element of alarm in regard to Origen's viewpoint is not diminished if we consider his use of the word historia in dealing with the New Testament. He is aware that Greek historians tell

---

[1] Man and Time (Papers from the Eranos Yearbooks 3, New York, 1957), p. 53 n19.
[2] See the definitions by Hanson, Allegory and Event, p 7.

true stories about voluntary self-sacrifice, about scholars in exile, about the work of evil spirits, and about the life of the Cynic philosopher Crates.[1] Origen is really interested in their work not as history but as a quarry for moral examples. He thus resembles, and is, a rhetorician or a philosopher rather than a historian. To be sure, he finds history valuable when it confirms the Bible. In this regard his most useful source was the work of Josephus, whose writings he employs more fully than those of any other historian.[2] Indeed, it would appear that sometimes when Origen speaks of history in a rather vague way he has Josephus in mind. Probably this is the case when he says that history tells us nothing about a forty-six year period in which the temple was being built, and almost nothing about the office held by the "royal officer" of John 4.46.[3] It is not clear, however, how he can say that it is clear from history that after the coming of Jesus there was no king of the Jews;[4] he is obviously neglecting the reign of Agrippa I (A.D. 37-44).

A special case is provided by his statement that there is no historical record of anyone's having encountered a "griffin".[5] Certainly Herodotus thought the griffin was mythical, but Origen's mind changed on the subject. In writing against Celsus he finally accepted its existence. Here as elsewhere, when Origen wanted to insist upon allegorization he could claim that something mentioned in scripture was not a historical phenomenon; if he was not concerned with allegory he could admit historicity. In the latter sense the gospels and Acts, in his view, do contain history.[6]

His main concern, however, is with the non-historical meaning. The unhistorical parts of scripture point beyond themselves to a spiritual meaning; indeed, everywhere the true meaning lies "beyond the history".[7] The exegete's mind must be "released

[1] *J* 6, 54, p. 163; *J* 13, 13, p. 285; *J* 28, 19, p. 413; *M* 15, 15, p. 391.
[2] Cf. G. Bardy, "Le souvenir de Josèphe chez les Pères". *Revue d'histoire ecclésiastique*, 43 (1948), p. 181.
[3] *J* 10, 28, p. 213; *J* 13, 58, p. 288.   [4] *P* 4, 1, 3, p. 296.
[5] *P* 4, 3, 2, p. 326; cf. *Miracle and Natural Law* (Amsterdam, 1952), p. 202.
[6] *P* 4, 3, 4, p. 329; *J* 6, 33, p. 143; *M* 15, 15, p. 392.
[7] *P* 4, 2.8—3.5, pp. 320-1; *J* 10, 22, p. 194; 10, 26, p. 199; 10, 40, p. 217.

from historical materials", for these provide nothing but a "stepping-stone".[1] Examples found in the commentaries on John and on Matthew alike reflect Origen's latent contempt for what he sometimes calls "mere history".[2] In view of this attitude, it is hard to see how he can criticize "the heterodox" for "rejoicing in allegories and referring the history about the healings to therapies of the soul".[3] Their method, and some of their results, are his own.

A sentence in the *Commentary on John* reveals one of the contemporary consequences of Origen's allegorization. "People marvel at Jesus", he says, "when they look into the history about him, but they no longer believe when the deeper meaning is disclosed to them; instead, they suppose it to be false."[4] Origen is obviously criticizing the literal-minded believer who cannot see any justification for allegorization or the consequent allegory. And if we consider the passages which Origen allegorizes in the gospels we are likely to share the literalist's view. As Hanson says, "Origen approached the Bible . . . with a series of presuppositions in his mind which had nothing particular to do with the thought of the Bible itself."[5] Because of this fact, it was necessary for him to insist that the texts often meant what they did not say.

To some extent Origen's position can be defended on the ground that there is a considerable element of ambiguity in language, even in the language of historians, and that many biblical texts are susceptible of more than one interpretation. To say this, however, is to miss the point that Origen was insisting not upon ambiguity as such but upon the correctness of his own spiritual interpretation. The method he employed meant that first he took a text with overwhelming literalness and then, having found some difficulty, proceeded in the direction of an equally overwhelming allegorization. The result was that while verbally he retained an outline (though not a very clear one) of the life and

---

[1] *J* 10, 5, p. 175; 20, 3, p. 329.
[2] In the late *M* 16, 12, p. 510; for the "mereness" of history cf. the rhetorician Theodore of Gadara, cited above, p. 73.
[3] *J* 20, 20, p. 352.   [4] *J* 20, 30, p. 368.   [5] *Allegory and Event*, p. 369.

teaching of Jesus, his central concern was with the "spiritual meaning" he found in it.

To assess the significance of his analysis is exceedingly difficult, since (1) he obviously valued John most highly among the apostolic writers, and (2) John himself points toward the appropriation of theological truth as a post-resurrection process. The gospels were written by men who were both remembering Jesus and discovering what he meant. Thus after Peter's vision (Acts 10.9–15), "the Spirit of Truth who was leading Peter into 'all the truth' (John 16.13) told him the 'many things' which he could not bear while Jesus was still with him according to the flesh".[1] Origen found that the tradition of the Church, as he understood it, pointed away from primitive misunderstandings of Jesus through John's more symbolical interpretation to his own exegesis. The basic ground on which Origen's view can be criticized is that he treated both John and himself as somehow exempt from the conditions of space and time or, in brief, of history. Origen confuses his own understanding of John not only with what the evangelist himself may have intended but also, on the other hand, with Truth itself. While his understanding is partly justified by John's love of symbolism and double meanings, it is a question whether the symbols point beyond themselves in the direction in which Origen was looking; and the gospel itself must be interpreted in relation to its own historical environment, which is not Platonic but Jewish (whether Palestinian or Hellenistic).

In the work of Origen and his predecessors we find an attempt to solve the problem presented to the Church by the existence of the four gospels. In varying ways, as we have seen, they tried to use the best literary and historical methods of their time. It cannot be said that they solved the problem or that they were able to write a life of Jesus. What remains significant in their work is not any solution. It is the fact that they did face the problem and tried to solve it. In this respect, and perhaps in this respect alone, their work has lasting significance.

At one point it is clear that Origen, at least, could perhaps have gone on beyond his rather formal literary and historical

[1] C 2, 2, p. 129.

methods. We have already seen that he was aware, in a rather literalistic way, that Jesus revealed himself in different ways to different persons, and that he correlated this variety with the different witnesses' levels of spiritual apprehension. But Origen was also aware of differences on a more simply human level. He could speak of the generic likeness of men as men and then go on to suggest that there are specific differences not only external but also mental. Paul was Paul; Peter was Peter and not Paul. Such differences extended even to the ways in which Peter and Paul would write the letter Alpha. And the specific content of various Christian virtues varied in relation to the person who wrote of them.[1] Had Origen further considered this point, and had he related it to the nature of the various books of the New Testament and their historical background, he would have gone far in the direction of modern critical and theological study.

He did not take this step, however, and we must therefore be content to see in his thought—as in that of the early Church generally—not final conclusions but elements which, combined in new ways and supplemented by other considerations, can be used in creating a more adequate understanding of the life of Jesus.

[1] *Num. hom.* 2, 2, pp. 10–12 Baehrens; cf. *O* 24, 2, pp. 353–4.

GLOSSARY

This section deals with four of the principal terms used by Graeco-Roman writers in analysing narratives: ἀπομνημόνευμα, ἱστορία, μῦθος, and πλάσμα (for some of these terms, and others, cf. *The Letter and the Spirit*, pp. 120–42). For the method of citation cf. p. vii.

1. Ἀπομνημόνευμα, ἀπομνημονεύειν

According to the rhetorician Theon, an ἀπομνημόνευμα is ⟨the record of⟩ an action or a subject with practical significance (βιοφελής, 96, 23). In other words, it is chiefly a longer χρεία (K. von Fritz in Pauly-Wissowa, *RE* Suppl. VI, pp. 87–9). The word implies an emphasis on the reliability of the record, since it is often used of "memoirs" written by witnesses (e.g., Xenophon on Socrates; cf. E. Schwartz in *RE* II, pp. 170–1; J. Weiss, *Das älteste Evangelium*, Göttingen, 1903, pp. 6–22). The genitive with the noun usually, though not always, refers to the subject of the memoirs rather than to their author. Justin, speaking of the gospels, classifies them as ἀπομνημόνευματα "of the apostles" or "composed by the apostles and their followers" (*Dial.* 103; also, *passim* in *Dial.* 100–7; *Apol.* 1, 66, 3, cf. 33, 5). The ἀπομνημόνευματα of Peter (*Dial.* 106) are probably the gospel of Mark, according to tradition composed by the apostle's disciple. Justin's follower Tatian apparently used the word in the same way (*Or.* 21, p. 23, 18 Schwartz; cf. 23, 7–8). The noun is not found frequently in early Christian literature; it occurs in Clement, *Str.* 2, 118, 3, in the singular to refer to the "memorial", a gnomic command, which Nicolaitan gnostics had received from their founder, and in Origen, *C* 7, 54, p. 204, in the plural to indicate what, in relation to the words of Heracles, his admirers cannot supply. In these instances the noun undoubtedly points toward the aspect of reminiscence.

The use of the verb is somewhat different. It occurs in Papias' defence of Mark, who "was not wrong when he wrote down single items ὡς ἀπομνημόνευσεν—as he remembered them, or in the form in which he recorded them?" The meaning of Papias' sentence (Eusebius, *H.E.* 3. 39, 15) seems unclear. When Justin (*Apol.* 1, 33, 5) says that the apostles were οἱ ἀπομνημονεύσαντες everything about the Saviour, he probably has in mind both recalling and recording. Similarly in two passages in Clement (*Protr.* 79, 3; *Str.* 5, 82, 4) both meanings are to be found, the first in regard to Clement himself, the second in regard to Luke's work in Acts (Paul at Athens). Two other passages, however, use the word primarily to mean "record"; speaking of his gnostic knowledge, Clement says that "there are some things not recorded by us" (*Str.* 1, 14, 2); and he says that Aristotle "records that Zaleukos . . . received the laws from Athena" (*Str.* 1, 170, 3). In neither case can the primary meaning be that of remembering.

Similarly the passages cited by Weiss (op. cit., p. 8 n1) from Irenaeus do not prove his contention that ἀπομνημονεύειν indicates remembering. Its Latin equivalent *meminit* is used twice of the evangelist John and his gospel (*Adv. haer.* 2, 22, 3, p. 328; 4, 10, 1, p. 172; cf. *commemoratus est,* 4, 2, 3, p. 148), but it is also used of Luke (5, 21, 2, p. 383). Of course Luke could have remembered Paul's teaching, in Irenaeus' view, but it would seem more likely that what is emphasized is recording. On the other hand, Weiss also cites Irenaeus' *Epistle to Florinus* (Eusebius, *H.E.* 5, 20, 6), and there ἀπομνημόνευεν means both recall and relate but not record.

Origen uses the verb of the author of Hebrews (Eusebius, *H.E.* 6, 25, 13) and of the evangelists (*J* 6, 34, p. 143; 10, 3, p. 172; *M* 16, 12, p. 510). In each instance the verb is related to remembering, but the aspect of remembering is explicitly stated separately. Therefore the primary meaning of ἀπομνημονεύειν for Origen is to record, not to recall.

2. Ἱστορία

Ἱστορία, according to Theon, is a systematically constructed narration (60, 6), and a narrative is an account which sets forth events which took place or as if they took place (78, 15). Most grammarians and rhetoricians distinguished history from both myth and πλάσμα (q. v.). But in Theon's definition all are treated as forms of history. A similar treatment is given by the grammarian Asclepiades (Sextus Empiricus, *Adv. math.* 1, 252–3). There are three kinds of history: true (factual), false (πλάσματα and myths), and like the true (as in comedy and mimes). True history deals with (1) the persons of gods, heroes, and famous men, (2) places and times, and (3) actions. (For the rhetorical analysis based on such subjects cf. pp. 39–44.)

The noun does not occur in the New Testament or the apostolic fathers, though the verb ἱστορεῖν, in the sense of "make acquaintance" is found in Gal. 1.18 and perhaps in Ignatius, *Eph.* 1, 2. The apologist Aristides (13, 7) raises the question of whether the Greek histories are mythical, "natural", or allegorical. Justin uses the verb to mean "relate" or "recount", in regard to Greek stories of the gods (*Apol.* 1, 21, 4; 22, 4; *Dial.* 69, 2), to a narrative by Moses (*Apol.* 1, 53, 8), and to his own statements (*Dial.* 62, 2). Tatian uses the noun of Greek and oriental writings (*Or.* 1, p. 1, 11 Schwartz; 31, p. 32, 21 [correct chronology required for truth in history]; 36, p. 38, 6 and 14; 37, p. 38, 20; 39, p. 40, 1) and of Hebrew-Christian history (40, p. 41, 11). Athenagoras uses the noun of Greek histories (*Leg.* 20, 3; 26, 1; 29, 1; 30, 4). The same use is found in Theophilus (*Ad Autol.* 2, 1–2.6; 3, 2 [useless histories of Herodotus and Thucydides]).

Their contemporary Lucian wrote a treatise on *How History is to be Written*; in it he stated that history must not contain an invocation of the Muses (10) and must avoid the myth and the encomium, as well as the hyperboles contained in both (8). Its "only goal is utility, which comes from truth alone" (9).

For Origen's use of history cf. pp. 114–16 above.

3. Μῦθος

The rhetoricians ordinarily differentiated history (no. 2), myth, and πλάσμα or fiction (no. 4). History is an account of what did take place; myth is an account of what could not take place; fiction is an account of what did not take place (Sextus Empiricus, *Adv. math.* 1, 263–4; cf. P. de Lacy in *American Journal of Philology* 69, 1948, pp. 267–8). Sometimes, however, myth and fiction were treated together and regarded as consisting of the genealogies of gods and heroes (Asclepiades in Sextus Empiricus 1, 252–3); such an analysis meant that stories of the gods could be treated as history. "Fictioned myth" or "to fiction a myth" (μῦθον πλάσσειν) is a common expression after Plato (*Tim.* 26 e); cf. Palaephatus, *Incred.*, *passim*; Philo, *Exsecr.* 162; Theon 75, 11 and 32; Hippolytus, *Ref.* 6, 19, 4; Origen, *M* 17, 30, p. 670. In any event, myths were not true, even though they might "portray truth" (Theon 59, 21; 72, 28; Aphthonius, II, 21, 2; cf. Nicolaus, III, 453.19—455.5) or provide guidance for the conduct of life (Hermogenes 3, 11 Spengel, 2, 4 Rabe). In the opinion of some analysts, myth was characteristic of tragedy, fiction, or comedy (Quintilian, *Inst. Or.* 2, 4, 2; cf. Dio Chrysostom, *Or.* 11, 7; Diogenes Laertius 5, 88; "tragic myth" of Valentinus, Hippolytus, *Ref.* 6, 42, 2).

The falsity of myths is emphasized in the Pastoral Epistles (1 Tim. 4.7; 2 Tim. 4.4; Tit. 1.14, "Jewish"; 1 Tim. 1.4, associated with genealogies, as above) and in 2 Peter (1.16; "follow" as in Josephus, *Ant.* 1, 22). The word "myth" does not occur in the apostolic fathers, but in Ignatius, *Magn.* 8, 1, we find "the ancient useless μυθεύματα"; the ending of the word implies the artificiality of the myths' origin. (Clement could hardly be expected to use the word when he treats the story of the phoenix as historical, 25, 1 and 5.) Among the apologists myths are uniformly regarded as false, and both Aristides and Tatian complain about allegorical exegesis of them (cf. W. den Boer in *VC* 1, 1947, pp. 156–8). Similarly Hippolytus, in his *Refutatio*, always uses the word in relation to the false stories told by Greeks, barbarians, and gnostics.

For Origen cf. pp. 65–6. Note that the object of heterodox worship is "a fiction (πλάσμα) and not truth, a myth and not mysteries" (*J* 13, 17, p. 241). Cf. also the note of Hanson, *Allegory and Event*, p. 276 n3.

4. Πλάσμα

In rhetoric the word means "fiction", a narrative which is lifelike but untrue, though as we have seen (no. 3) it was not always sharply differentiated from myth. One man's myth was another man's πλάσμα. In its rhetorical sense it does not occur in the New Testament, the apostolic fathers, or the apologists. Origen regards the Sadducees' story of the woman with seven husbands (Matt. 22.25–8) as either a myth (*L* 39, p. 226; *M* 17, 30, p. 670, 22) or a fiction (*M* p. 670, 28; 17, 33, p. 688). In writing against Celsus, who had said (*C* 3, 27, p. 224) that the gospels contained myths and πλάσματα, Origen argues only that the gospel stories are not πλάσματα (1, 40, p. 90; 2, 10–11, pp. 138–9; 2, 13, p. 141; 2, 15, p. 144; 2, 26, p. 155; 2, 48, p. 169; 2, 56, pp. 180–1; 3, 33, p. 229, possibly because his allegorical method still requires him to treat some of them as myths, but more probably because he is combining myth with fiction (cf. 1, 42, pp. 92–3, where "impossible" stories are called πλάσματα).

APPENDIX

ORIGEN'S EXEGETICAL WRITINGS ON THE GOSPELS

Six of Origen's works are especially significant for his exegesis of the gospels.

(1) His treatise *De principiis* (*P*) is extant in some Greek fragments, which include most of the fourth book (on inspiration and exegesis), in a Latin translation (and edition) made by Rufinus in 397, and in Latin fragments of a more literal translation made by Jerome in 398. The text was edited (along with passages from the anathematisms of the council of Constantinople in 553) by Paul Koetschau in 1913 (*Die griechischen christlichen Schriftsteller der drei ersten Jahrhunderten, Origenes Werke* V, Berlin). There is an English translation by G. Butterworth, *Origen on First Principles* (London, 1936).

(2) His *Commentary on John* (*J*) has largely been preserved in two manuscripts of the thirteenth and fourteenth centuries, edited with Greek fragments by Erwin Preuschen in 1903 (*GCS* IV). The contents of the books are as follows:

Book I on John 1.1 (pp. 3–51)
  II John 1.1–7 (pp. 52–97)
  III (lost)
  IV fragments (pp. 98–9)
  V fragments (pp. 100–5)
  VI John 1.19–29 (pp. 106–69; end lost)
 VII–IX (lost)
  X John 2.12–25 (pp. 170–225)
 XI–XII (lost)
  XIII John 4.13–54 (pp. 226–97)
 XIV–XVIII (lost)
  XIX John 8.19–25 (pp. 298–326; beginning and
    end lost)

XX	John 8.37–53 (pp. 327–88)
XXI–XXVII	(lost)
XXVIII	John 11.39–57 (pp. 389–424)
XXIX–XXXI	(lost)
XXXII	John 13.2–33 (pp. 425–80)

The average number of *GCS* pages for complete books is about 50, and it thus appears that the whole work would have contained about 1600 pages. Not all of it was equally significant. Origen naturally expounded the prologue more fully than he did later sections of John; the first ten books, indeed, average about $6\frac{1}{2}$ pages of exegesis per verse. But the last twenty-two books cannot have contained more than about two pages of exegesis per verse. It is highly probable that Origen never wrote more than thirty-two books.

(3) *The Homilies on Luke* (*L*) are preserved in a Latin translation made by Jerome and in Greek fragments. The oldest manuscript of the Latin version comes from the ninth century. M. Rauer edited the text in 1930 (*GCS* IX).

(4) The treatise *De oratione* (*O*) survives in one Greek manuscript of the fourteenth century, which was edited by Koetschau in 1899 (*GCS* II). It contains, among other things, exegesis of the Lord's Prayer.

(5) The *Commentary on Matthew* (*M*) is preserved in two ways. (a) In Greek, in addition to fragments, we possess books X–XVII (on Matt. 13.36—22.33) in three manuscripts of the thirteenth and fourteenth centuries; these were edited by Erich Klostermann in 1935 (*GCS* X). (b) There is also a Latin version of the sixth or seventh century; it begins with XII 9 (Matt. 16.12) and continues to the end of the gospel. The oldest manuscripts of this version come from the ninth and tenth centuries; it was edited by Klostermann in 1933 (*GCS* XI). The edition was completed with fragments, indices, and essays by Klostermann, E. Benz, and L. Früchtel in 1941–55 (*GCS* XII). The exegesis is disposed as follows:

Book X on Matt. 13.36—14.15 (pp. 1–34 Klostermann)
XI Matt. 14.15—15.39 (pp. 34–69)

XII   Matt. 16.1—17.9 (pp. 69–170)
XIII   Matt. 17.10—18.18 (pp. 170–271)
XIV   Matt. 18.19—19.11 (pp. 271–348)
XV   Matt. 19.12—20.16 (pp. 348–461)
XVI   Matt. 20.17—21.22 (pp. 461–574)
XVII   Matt. 21.23—22.33 (pp. 575–703)

It will be seen that Books X and XI are considerably shorter than the others, and by comparing the formulas with which Origen concluded books of the early *Commentary on John* and Book VI of the late *Contra Celsum*, Klostermann was able to show that the *Commentary on Matthew* has been abbreviated. The Latin translation begins at Comm. XII, 9 (on Matt. 16.13), p. 80, and continues after the Greek ends.

Ser. comm. 1–23 on Matt. 22.34–23.39 (pp. 1–54)
            29–62   Matt. 24.1–51 (pp. 55–145)
            63–73   Matt. 25.1–46 (pp. 145–74)
            74–114   Matt. 26.1–75 (pp. 174–241)
            115–145   Matt. 27.1–66 (pp. 241–99)

(6) The Greek text of *Contra Celsum* (*C*) was edited from two fourteenth-century manuscripts by Paul Koetschau in 1899 (*GCS* I–II). Recent papyrological discoveries have not contributed as much as had been expected; see J. Scherer, *Extraits des livres I et II du Contre Celse d'Origène* (Cairo, 1956). There is an excellent English translation by H. Chadwick, *Origen: Contra Celsum* (Cambridge, 1953).

BIBLIOGRAPHY

Since full bibliographies on ancient exegesis can be found in *The Letter and the Spirit* (London, 1957) and in J. Pépin, *Mythe et allégorie* (Paris, 1958), this list includes only works fairly closely related to the work of Origen.

GENERAL

DE FAYE, E. *Clément d'Alexandrie*, Paris, 1898.
PRAT, F. *Origène le théologue et l'exégète*, Paris, 1907.
BAUER, W. *Das Leben Jesu im Zeitalter der neutestamentlichen Apokryphen*, Tübingen, 1909.
BIGG, C. *The Christian Platonists of Alexandria*, 2nd ed., Oxford, 1913.
TOLLINTON, R. B. *Clement of Alexandria*, London, 1914.
DE FAYE, E. *Origène, sa vie, son œuvre, sa pensée*, Paris, 1923–8.
SMITH, H. *Ante-Nicene Exegesis of the Gospels*, London, 1925–9.
CADIOU, R. *La jeunesse d'Origène*, Paris, 1935.
MOLLAND, E. *The Conception of the Gospel in the Alexandrian Theology*, Oslo, 1938.
DEN BOER, W. *De allegorese in het werk van Clemens Alexandrinus*, Leiden, 1940.
MONDÉSERT, C. *Clément d'Alexandrie*, Paris, 1944.
CAMELOT, T. *Foi et gnose . . . chez Clément d'Alexandrie*, Paris, 1945.
DANIÉLOU, J. *Origène*, Paris, 1948.
DE LUBAC, H. *Histoire et Esprit*, Paris, 1950.
CHADWICK, H. *Origen: Contra Celsum*, Cambridge, 1953.
HANSON, R. P. C. *Allegory and Event*, London, 1959.
WILES, M. F. *The Spiritual Gospel*, Cambridge, 1960.

SPECIAL

BORST, J. *Beiträge zur sprachlich-stilistischen und rhetorischen Würdigung des Origenes*, Freising, 1913.
HARNACK, A. *Der kirchengeschichtliche Ertrag der exegetischen Arbeiten des Origenes, Texte und Untersuchungen* 42, 3–4 (Leipzig, 1918–19).
STREIBER, E. "Einiges zur Schriftauslegung des Origenes", *Internationale kirchliche Zeitschrift* 13 (1923), pp. 145–69.
BARDY, G. "Les traditions juives dans l'œuvre d'Origène", *Revue biblique* 34 (1925), pp. 217–52.

CADIOU, R. "Dictionnaires antiques dans l'œuvre d'Origène", *Revue des études grecques* 45 (1932), pp. 271–85.

KLOSTERMANN, E. "Ueberkommene Definitionen im Werke des Origenes", *Zeitschrift für die neutestamentliche Wissenschaft* 37 (1938), pp. 54–61.

KLOSTERMANN, E. "Formen der exegetischen Arbeiten des Origenes", *Theologische Literatur-Zeitung* 72 (1947), pp. 203–8.

BERTRAND, F. *Mystique de Jésus chez Origène*, Paris, 1951.

LÄUCHLI, S. "The Polarity of the Gospels in the Exegesis of Origen", *Church History* 21 (1952), pp. 215–4.

LÄUCHLI, S. "Die Frage nach der Objektivität der Exegese des Origenes", *Theologische Zeitschrift* 10 (1954), pp. 178–97.

DANIÉLOU, J. "Origène comme exégète de la Bible", *Texte und Untersuchungen* 63 (Berlin, 1957), pp. 280–90.

PÉPIN, J. "A propos de l'histoire de l'exégèse allégorique: l'absurdité, signe d'allégorie", *Texte und Untersuchungen* 63 (Berlin, 1957), pp. 395–413.

INDEXES

EXEGETICAL TERMS

αἴνιγμα, 52n, 66, 87
ἀλληγορία, 52n
ἀναγωγή, 63, 74 (verb)
ἀνασκευή, 40–7, 67, 87, 110, 114
ἀπίθανον, 41
ἀπομνημόνευμα, (and verb), 15, 17, 18, 20, 27, 54, 119–20
γνωμή, 15, 19, 98–9
διήγημα, διήγησις, 15, 102
ἱστορία, 114–16, 120–1

κατασκευή, 40 46, 70–1, 73–7
μῦθος, 40–7, 65–6, 87, 121–2
ὁμοίωσις, 103
πιθανότης, 40
πλάσμα, (71–4), 122–3
σαφήνεια, 102
σύνταξις, 17–18
τερατολογία, 20
τόπος, 40
χρεία, 14, 17–18, 99–101, 119

Matthew
3.4 (Clement), 35n
4.12 (Tatian), 26n
4.12–6 (Tatian), 25
4.17–22 (Tatian), 26n
5.1 (Tatian), 26
5.3,6 (Clement), 35–6
9.9 (Tatian), 26n
11.1 (Tatian), 25
11.12–9 (Tatian), 25
11.30 (Justin), 21
16.4 (Justin), 19
19.16–30 (Tatian), 25
20.1–16 (Tatian), 25
22.1–14 (Titian), 25
26.17 (Clement), 37

Mark
1.14–20 (Tatian), 26n
3.16–7 (Justin), 20
4.33–4 (Theodotus), 13
6.12–3 (Tatian), 25
10.17–31 (Tatian), 25; (Clement), 37
15.21–5 (Basilides), 10

Luke
1.1–3 (Justin), 20; 1.1–5 (Tatian), 26
3.1 (Irenaeus), 34; 3.1—4.31 (Marcion), 11
3.19–20 (Tatian), 25
3.23 (Melito), 30; (Irenaeus), 34
4.14–22 (Tatian), 26n
5.1–11 (Tatian), 26n
6.17 (Tatian), 26
8.2 (Celsus), 76n
9.51–6 (Tatian), 25
9.62 (Justin), 21
10.38–42 (Tatian), 25
12.13–21 (Tatian), 25
13.6–9 (Marcion), 34

14.1–24 (Tatian), 25
14.45—15.11 (Tatian), 68n
16.14–27 (Tatian), 25
17.5–6 (Marcion), 34
18.18–30 (Tatian), 25
19.29–46 (Marcion), 11

John
1.1–3 (Theophilus), 30; 1.1—2.1 (Alogi), 28
1.14 (Alogi), 28n
1.15–7 (Heracleon), 13
2.1–11 (Theodotus), 13; 2.11 (Tatian), 23
2.13 (Alogi), 28; (Melito), 30; 2.13–25 (Tatian), 23
3.1–21 (Tatian), 23–4; 3.3 (Tatian), 26n; 3.3,7 (Alogi), 28n
3.22–4 (Tatian), 26
4.4–45 (Tatian), 24; 4.24 (Tatian), 25
5.1–47 (Tatian), 24
6.4 (Alogi), 28; (Melito), 30
7.2–31 (Tatian), 25
8.50 (Tatian), 24
8.56–7 (Irenaeus), 34
11.55 (Melito), 30
12 (Tatian), 24
13 (Clement), 37; (Tatian), 24
14.26 (Theophilus), 30
16.25,29 (Theodotus), 31
18.28 (Clement), 37
19.19–24 (Tatian), 24
19.39 (Tatian), 24
21.24 (Muratorian fragment), 31
1 Cor. 11.23 (Marcion), 12
2 Cor. 12 (Marcion), 12
Gal. 2.5 (Irenaeus), 32
Col 4.4 (Irenaeus), 32
2 Tim. 4.14 (Irenaeus), 32
Rev. 4.7 (Irenaeus), 33

BIBLICAL PASSAGES INTERPRETED BY ORIGEN

Genesis

1.28	88	26.3	95
8.7	82	26.6–13	67
		26.22	95
Isaiah		26.39,42	94
30.26	108	26.57	95
46.4	82	27.32–54	96–7
		28.2	77
Matthew		28.30	109
1.1	82		
1.18	82	*Mark*	
1.25	82, 109	1.3	84
3.2	98	4.30	103
3.11	98	4.34	102
4.4	62	5.2	89–90
4.8	63	5.21–43	89
4.17	39, 98	7.24–30	89
5.29–30	99, 107n	9.2	80
5.39	99	9.14–29	89
6.9–13	100–1	10.1–16	92
8.5–13	87, 89	10.19	60
8.28	89–90	10.35	108, 113
9.18–26	89	10.46–52	92–3
13.24–30	102	13.27	109
13.36–43	102	13.35	107–8
13.44–50	103	14.3–9	67
13.53–4	104	14.10,19	95
15.21–8	89	14.60–3	95
15.32–9	88	15.21–33	95–7
16.8	55	15.44–5	98
16.18–19	91–2	16.5	77
16.20–1	57		
16.28	109	*Luke*	
17.2	80	1.1	53
17.14–21	89	1.17	98
18.2–3	106	2.41–52	83–4
18.18	92	3.1,23	83
18.23–35	104	3.18	84n
19.1–15	92	3.22	73
19.12	106	4.5	63
19.19	60	4.31	85
19.27	110	7.1–10	89
19.29	108	7.11–17	74
20.1–16	105	7.36–50	67
20.20	108	8.27	89–90
20.29–34	92–3	8.40–56	89
21.9	55	8.49–56	74
24.29	108	8.52	75
24.30–1	109	9.29	80
25.34	109	9.37–43	89
		9.60	107

Luke (cont.)

10.4	99, 107
10.29–37	105
11.2–4	100–1
12.6	107
14.12	107
15.21	105
16.22–3	106
18.15–17	92
18.20	60
18.34–43	93
22.3–4	95
23.26	95–6
23.33–4	96
23.44–5	96–7
24.4	77
24.16	80
24.39	(not quoted), 78
24.43	78

John

1.1	56
1.28	84, 87
2.12–16	85–6
4.1–2	86
4.6,10	56n
4.35	86
4.43–5	86–7
4.46–54	86–7, 89, 115
5.2–9	89
6.1	84
6.3	89n
6.9	88
6.53	88
11.1–44	74
11.18	84n
12.1–8	67
13.25	56n
14.6	102
14.12	75
16.13	117
17.3	56

17.24	109n
19.17	95–6
20.12	77
20.22	91
20.25	56
20.25–7	76
21.20	56n
21.25	102

Acts

10.9–15	117

Rom.

8.35—9.1	57

1 Cor.

2.2	91
9.27	57

2 Cor.

3.6	88
4.8–10	57
8.18	56
11.6	56

Gal.

5.17	57

Eph.

1.4	109n

Phil.

3.11–13	57

1 Thess.

5.2	107

Heb.

4.3	109n

1 Pet.

5.13	55

ANCIENT AUTHORS OR LITERATURE

A. PAGAN
Aphthonius, 45–6, 122
Aristaenetus, 50n
Arrian, 48–9
Asclepiades, 121
Celsus, 59–60, 70–8, 94, 123
Chaeremon, 83
Cicero, 67n
Cocondrius, 103n
Dio Chrysostom, 44–5, 71–2, 122
Diogenes Laertius, 122
Hermogenes, 14n, 15, 17n, 19, 40,
    45, 66, 122
Lucian, 39, 121
Nicolaus, 122
Orphic literature, 47
Palaephatus, 72n, 122
Plato, 122
Polybius of Sardis, 103n
Porphyry, 51
Quintilian, 15, 40, 122
Sextus Empiricus, 47–8, 66n, 121
Strabo, 71n
Theodore of Gadara, 40, 116n
Theon (Aelius), 14n, 15, 17n, 18n,
    40–5, 58–9, 65–6, 72n, 99–100,
    119–22
Trypho, 101, 103
Xenophon, 20, 119

B. JEWISH
Josephus, 69, 115, 122
Philo, 56n, 62, 81n, 106, 122

C. CHRISTIAN*
Alogi, 28
Apollinaris of Hierapolis, 30

Aristides, 121–2
Athenagoras, 121
Clement of Alexandria, 23, 30,
    35–7, 47, 50, 57, 62, 64n, 80,
    119–20
Clement of Rome, 122
Epiphanius, 28
Eustathius, 74
Gaius of Rome, 28–9, 59, 61
Gregory Thaumaturgus, 51–2
Hippolytus, 29, 62, 122
Ignatius, 121–2
Irenaeus, 13n, 21n, 23, 32–5, 82,
    87n, 104n, 105n, 120
Julius Africanus, 39, 81
Justin, 14, 16, 19–22, 119–21
Melito, 29–30
Muratorian fragment, 30–2
Papias, 14–19, 21–2, 32, 36
Sextus, 106
Tatian, 22–8, 37n, 47, 60–1, 68n,
    88, 119, 121–2
Theophilus of Antioch, 30, 121

D. GNOSTIC/SECTARIAN
Basilides, 10
Carpocratians, 104
Cerinthus, 33
Ebionites, 55n, 60
Heracleon, 13, 62, 87
Marcion, Marcionites, 10–12, 34, 39,
    59n, 60
Montanists, 28–9
Quartadecimans, 29–30, 37
Theodotus, 12–13
Valentinians, 12–13, 34, 87

* Eusebius and Origen are omitted because their names occur so frequently.

Audet, J.-P., 39n
Aulitsky, 51n

Bardy, G., 115n
Bauer, W., 80n, 93n, 95n, 107n
Benz, E., 125
Bertrand, F., 81n., 95n, 102n, 104n, 106n, 111–12
Bidez, J., 51n
Brown, R. E., 6n
Buckley, E. R., 22n
Bultmann, R., 6
Butterworth, G., 124

Cadiou, R., 51, 52n, 101n
Capelle, W., 51n
Casey, R. P., 6n
Chadwick, H., ix, 2n, 71n, 106n, 124
Cross, F. M., Jr, 6n
Cullmann, O., 11n

D'Alès, A., 29n
Daniélou, J., ix, 85n, 87n, 105
De Jonge, M., 6n
De Lacy, P., 122
Den Boer, W., 36n
Diels, H., 101n

Früchtel, L., 125

Gardner-Smith, P., 6n
Goodenough, E. R., 6n
Grant, F. C., 18n

Hanson, R. P. C., ix, 39n, 66n, 67n, 82n, 114n, 116, 122
Harnack, A. v., 11n, 34n, 55n, 85n

Jay, E. G., 100n
Jülicher, A., 19n, 28n

Klostermann, E., 51, 55n, 66n, 81n, 125–6
Koch, H., 31n
Koch, Hal, 112
Koetschau, P., 124, 126
Kraeling, C. H., 23
Kroll, W., 44

Laeuchli, S., ix
Lana, I., 40
Lohse, B., 29n, 30n

Metzger, B. M., 23n
Mondésert, C., 37n

Pease, A. S., 50n
Perkins, J. W., 29n
Pott, A., 23n
Preuschen, E., 23n, 124
Puech, H.-C., 114

Quasten, J., 21n, 31n

Rauer, M., 125
Reichardt, W., 81n
Reichel, G., 45

Scherer, J., 126
Schoedel, W. R., ix
Stegemann, W., 40n
Stendahl, K., 6n

Taylor, R. O. P., 17n
Toynbee, J., 29n

Van der Valk, M., 39n
Völker, W., 112n

Weinel, 18n
Windisch, H., 6n

Ziegler, K., 48
Zöllig, A., 112n